Lost Stations of
YORKSHIRE
Part 2: The North and East Ridings

Map showing the stations featured in Lost Stations of Yorkshire, Parts 1 and 2.

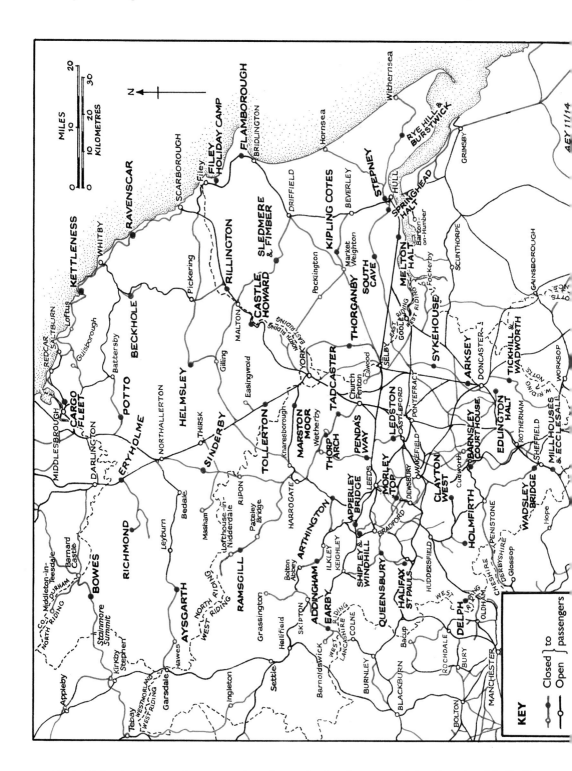

The highlighted stations on this map are those featured in *Lost Stations of Yorkshire*, Parts 1 and 2. *Alan Young*

Lost Stations of

YORKSHIRE

Part 2: The North and East Ridings

Alan Young

Silver Link Publishing Ltd

First published in 2015

British Library Cataloguing in Publication Data

A catalogue record for this book is available from the British Library.

ISBN 978 1 85794 453 2

Silver Link Publishing Ltd
The Trundle
Ringstead Road
Great Addington
Kettering
Northants NN14 4BW

Tel/Fax: 01536 330588
email: sales@nostalgiacollection.com
Website: www.nostalgiacollection.com

Printed and bound in the Czech Republic

The Author - Alan Young

Alan was born in Newcastle upon Tyne in 1951. After completing his A levels at George Stephenson Grammar School, West Moor, he read geography at Fitzwilliam College, Cambridge. For almost 40 years Alan taught geography, working in Hertfordshire, London and Lancashire. Having retired from teaching he is now a freelance Tour Manager who works with a railway holiday travel firm – one of the tours he leads is 'Yorkshire by Steam'.

While most railway enthusiasts collected engine numbers, Alan's interest was in the infrastructure, particularly stations. The first stations he remembers were on the 'Coast Circle' route between Newcastle and Whitley Bay. It might appear impertinent for a native of Northumberland to presume to write about stations in Yorkshire, but his earliest recollection of a train journey beyond Tyneside was a steam-hauled excursion to Leyburn in Yorkshire in about 1955. His interest in Yorkshire lines and stations was deepened by summer holidays based in Harrogate and Whitby, and frequent journeys on the East Coast Main Line between Newcastle and London, sometimes via Ripon on the 'Queen of Scots' Pullman.

Alan's passionate interest in geography developed as he became an avid collector of Ordnance Survey maps, then, starting with his purchase of a North Eastern Region timetable in 1962, he began to plan journeys to visit the region's lines and stations. Thanks to a level of trust that parents are not encouraged to show

in their children today, Alan used Runabout and 'Day Line Diesel' tickets to travel on routes that were soon to close as the Beeching cuts took effect, including the Richmond and Middleton-in-Teesdale branches. Alan's station photography began in 1962 at Blencow on the old Penrith-Keswick line, and it gathered momentum in the early 1970s spurred on by missing, by just a few days, the opportunity to photograph some Tyneside stations before they were demolished. He set out to visit all stations, past and present, in Great Britain and Ireland, and to photograph them in colour.

In 1974 Alan's first article was published in *Railway World*, and he shared his interest in disused stations in 'A British Closed Station Safari' published in *Railway Magazine* in 1980. He has written or contributed to books on railway architecture, railway mapping, private and untimetabled stations, British Railway station totems, and aspects of Tyneside, Northumberland and Yorkshire railways. His distinctive hand-drawn maps are found in various railway books including Richard Furness's 'Poster-to-Poster' series, for which he also provides editorial guidance. He is author of the companion volume in this series, *Lost Stations of Northumberland & Durham*. For some time he has supplied articles and photographs to the 'Disused Stations' website, for which he is also the cartographer, and provides support in editing and proof-reading material submitted for the website.

Contents

Acknowledgements

I am grateful for the generous help I have received from a number of people while preparing this book. I applaud Nick Catford's vision in setting up the 'Disused Stations' website, and he has worked to enhance the quality of the photographs in this book. Martin Bairstow is undoubtedly one of the best-informed authorities on the railways of Yorkshire; we have had many useful conversations, and he has provided access to his remarkable collection of railway photographs, including those taken by G. C. Lewthwaite. Martin's series of books on Yorkshire railways is prominent in the Bibliography, and guest contributors to his books, notably David R. Smith (Hull area), Stuart Carmichael (camping coaches on the Whitby-Loftus line) and John Farline (Filey Holiday Camp) have given detail on specific stations and train services.

Peter Tuffrey, with whom I collaborated on his *East Yorkshire Stations* book, has made his photographic collection available. Mark Dyson and Neil Cholmondeley have recently visited disused stations and taken photos specifically for this book. Richard Furness has supplied images of station totem signs.

Photographers who have been generous with their support and encouragement include Les Turnbull, David Mitchell and Brian Johnson; Michael Stewart and Brian Halford have supplied ticket images from their collections; Roy Lambeth has provided locomotive information; Paul Wright and Graham Larkbey have kindly read and commented on the manuscript; and finally John Mann's vast portfolio of photos that he collected or took himself, which was donated to the 'Disused Stations' website, has provided a number of excellent pictures.

Glossary

BR British Railways (1948-64)/British Rail (1965-94)

ECML East Coast Main Line (London-Doncaster-York-Newcastle-Edinburgh)

H&BR Hull & Barnsley Railway

LMS London Midland & Scottish Railway

LNER London & North Eastern Railway

L&YR Lancashire & Yorkshire Railway

NER North Eastern Railway

TUCC Transport Users' Consultative Committee

Bibliography

Addyman, John F. and Fawcett, Bill (eds) *A History of the Hull and Scarborough Railway* (NERA/Kestrel, 2013)

Bairstow, Martin *Railways in East Yorkshire* (3 volumes) (Author, 1995-2007)
    Railways Around Whitby, Vol 1 (Author, 2nd edition, 2008)
    Railways Around Harrogate (3 volumes) (Author, 1986-1998)

Baker, Stuart K. *Rail Atlas: Great Britain and Ireland* (OPC, 13th edition, 2013)

Beeching, Richard *The Reshaping of British Railways* (The 'Beeching Report') (HMSO, 1963)

Biddle, Gordon *Victorian Stations* (David & Charles, 1973)
    Britain's Historic Railway Buildings (Oxford University Press, 2003)

Bragg, S. and Scarlett, E. *North Eastern Lines and Stations* (NERA, 1999)

Burton, Warwick *The Malton & Driffield Junction Railway* (Martin Bairstow, 1998)

Chapman, Stephen (ed) *The Hull & Barnsley Railway* (Bellcode, 1999)

Clinker, C. R. *Register of Closed Passenger Stations and Goods Depots* (AvonAnglia, 1978)

Cook, R. A. and Hoole, Ken *North Eastern Railway Historical Maps* (RCHS, 2nd edition, 1991)

Croughton, Godfrey, Kidner, R. W. and Young, Alan *Private and Untimetabled Stations* (Oakwood Press, 1982)

Fawcett, Bill *A History of North Eastern Railway Architecture* (3 volumes) (NERA, 2001-05)
    George Townsend Andrews of York 'The Railway Architect' (Yorkshire Architectural & York Archaeological Society/NERA, 2011)

Gibbins, E. A. *The Railway Closure Controversy* (Leisure Products, 2000)

Hoole, Ken *A Regional History of the Railways of Great Britain*, Vol 4 *The North East* (David & Charles, 2nd edition, 1974)
    Railway Stations of the North East (David & Charles, 1985)

Howat, Patrick *The Railways of Ryedale* (Martin Bairstow, 2004)

Hurst, Geoffrey *Register of Closed Railways 1948-1991* (Milepost Publications, 1992)

Ludlam, A. J. *The Catterick Camp Military Railway and the Richmond Branch* (Oakwood Press, 1993)

Quick, Michael *Railway Passenger Stations in Great Britain: a chronology* (RCHS, 2009)

Rhodes, Simon M. *Ravenscar: the town that never was* (Smart Publications, 2nd edition, 1998)

Simmons, Jack *The Railway in Town and Country 1830-1914* (David & Charles, 1986)

Smith, Martin *Britain's Light Railways* (Ian Allan, 1994)

Stockwell, Jonathan and Drummond, Ian *Rails Along the Derwent* (Holne Publishing, 2013)

Teasdale, J. G. (ed) *A History of British Railways' North Eastern Region* (NERA, 2009)

Thompson, Michael *The Railways of Hull & East Yorkshire* (Hutton Press Ltd, 1992)

Tomlinson, W. W. *The North Eastern Railway* (1914; David & Charles reprint, 1967)

Tuffrey, Peter *East Yorkshire Railway Stations* (Amberley, 2012)

Turnbull, Les *Tickets not Transferable* (Ergo Press, 2007)

Walton, Peter *The Stainmore & Eden Valley Railways* (OPC, 1992)

White, H. P. *Forgotten Railways* (David & Charles, 1986)

Hansard (various) (HMSO)
North Eastern Express (various) (North Eastern Railway Society)

Introduction

Prior to the sweeping changes to county boundaries in 1974, Yorkshire was divided into three administrative units, the North, East and West Ridings – 'Riding' is derived from the Old English word 'thriding', meaning 'one third'. This volume and its companion, which covers the West Riding, are based on the traditional county; almost every station included in the survey was closed before the boundaries were reorganised.

The historic county of Yorkshire, prior to the changes to county boundaries, was by far the largest in England. Extending to 6,090 square miles, its nearest rival was Lincolnshire, at 2,663 square miles. The West Riding – at 2,768 square miles – was itself larger than Lincolnshire.

Within Yorkshire there were rich industrial resources, principally in the West Riding. Medieval monasteries owned vast acreages on which sheep were reared, providing wool that at first supplied handloom weavers, and from these beginnings grew the mills of Leeds, Bradford, Halifax, Huddersfield and many other centres. Long before the Industrial Revolution, iron ore and timber supplied small-scale iron foundries, which ultimately produced the world-famous steel industry of Sheffield and Rotherham. The rich pastures of the Dales supported dairying, while the Vale of York excelled in arable farming. On the coast fishing and trade with the continent brought prosperity to Hull and to a lesser extent to Scarborough and Whitby. From their birthplace in the 'Great Northern Coalfield' of Northumberland and Durham, railways spread into Yorkshire, where the growing industries and productive farmland offered lucrative traffic. The Vale of York provided a convenient routeway between London, the northern coalfield and Scotland, and the city of York developed a strategic role on this East Coast Main Line, which became one of the nation's principal passenger arteries; Doncaster also developed into a major railway centre. The railways (coupled with the provisions of the Bank Holidays Act of 1871) enabled Victorian citizens to enjoy recreation at the coast or at inland resorts, and by 1850 Whitby, Bridlington, Scarborough and Harrogate could all be reached by rail.

By the late 19th century the West Riding had acquired a dense and intricate network of lines as rival railway companies aspired to serve the industries and burgeoning population, enabling Britain's most productive 'York, Derby and Notts' coalfield to be exploited. In the North and East Ridings, apart from in the vicinity of Hull, the network was less complex, but every settlement of moderate importance was served. Railways enabled the remarkable growth of Middlesbrough on the Tees estuary, exploiting the local Cleveland iron ore and County Durham's coal. Routes were provided through the valleys of the North York Moors and along its coastal cliffs; two routes courageously crossed the lonely Wolds; and several made their way up the picturesque Pennine Dales, such as the line through Wensleydale between Northallerton, Leyburn, Hawes and Garsdale. Two of England's most famous lines – the Stainmore (Darlington-Penrith) and the Settle & Carlisle – uncompromisingly assaulted the Yorkshire Pennines, the former for sound economic reasons to convey iron ore between Cumberland and Teesside, and the latter springing from bad relations between rival railway companies. The Stainmore route has gone, but against all odds the Settle & Carlisle survives – and thrives. However, some significant gaps were left in the network. Schemes to build into upper Swaledale came to nothing, while the North Eastern Railway's intention of building a 'North Holderness' branch line to serve the countryside north-east of Beverley was abandoned in 1903 in favour of providing a bus service; but the company's tile wall maps, some of which survive, misleadingly show this line as built.

By the time of the First World War, although the North Eastern Railway enjoyed supremacy in the North and East Ridings, in the West Riding this company jostled for space with the Midland, Lancashire & Yorkshire, London & North Western, Great Northern, Great Central and Hull & Barnsley companies. At the 'Grouping' of 1923 Yorkshire's railways came under the control of the London & North Eastern and London Midland & Scottish companies, with a few minor lines (such as the Derwent Valley) retaining their independence. In the nationalised British Railways, created in 1948, Yorkshire's lines were allocated to three of the six regions – the North Eastern, Eastern, and London Midland – almost all of the North and East Riding lines being administered by the North Eastern.

The North and East Ridings of Yorkshire possessed a delightfully varied collection of passenger stations. The process of selecting them for this book, and for the companion volume covering the West Riding, was tantalising, as it was intended to include representatives of the different companies as well as stations large and small, urban and rural, elegant and austere, for public or restricted use, termini and through stations, and locations scattered across the county as far as its boundaries. Inevitably Dr Richard Beeching's name appears from time to time. As Chairman of the British Railways Board he was given the task of making the railways financially viable, and the *Reshaping of British Railways* report of March 1963 – its popular name of the 'Beeching Report' is used in the text – listed more than 2,300 stations for closure and identified services to be withdrawn or modified; there were also recommendations for the modernisation of freight transport. Popular mythology would have it that all closures were the outcome of the 'Beeching Axe', but it will be seen from the stations included in this book that Beeching merely accelerated a process of closures that had begun much earlier, and

some closures in the last 50 years (such as Flamborough and Cargo Fleet stations) were not actually recommended by Beeching.

As the title 'lost stations' implies, all have been closed to passenger traffic, but a strict definition of 'lost' is elusive. Some, such as Beckhole, have gone without trace, while others, such as Aysgarth, are superbly preserved. Between these extremes are locations such as Tollerton, where the passenger station has gone but associated structures remain, and Thorganby, where the main building survives but in an advanced state of decay.

This book is a companion to the popular 'Disused Stations' website, which now features more than 2,000 locations. A number of stations found on the website are included here, with rewritten text and, in some cases, different photographs to illustrate them, while others are new. They are arranged in order of opening.

'Yorkshire' defined

This book locates the individual station sites within Yorkshire as it existed prior to the local government reorganisation that took place on 1 April 1974. In fact, the counties and boundaries that were set in 1974 were for the purpose of creating administrative districts, and the historic counties were not altered.

In recent years many of the 1974 County Councils have themselves been swept away, confusing the situation even further. The author felt, therefore, that using the historic county would be easier for the reader.

STATION NAME	Indicates station closed to passengers pre-nationalisation
STATION NAME	Indicates station closed to passengers post-nationalisation
STATION NAME	Indicates station closed to passengers post-privatisation

BECKHOLE (1835)

Date opened	18 July 1835, by special arrangement; reopened July 1908
Location	Beside a track leading south-west from Beck Hole village
Company on opening	Whitby & Pickering Railway; reopened by North Eastern Railway
Date first closed to passengers	1 July 1865
Date closed completely	21 September 1914
Company on closing	North Eastern Railway (both closures)
Present state	Demolished
County	Yorkshire North Riding (now North Yorkshire)
OS grid ref	NZ821022

Pioneering railways had no precedents, and arrangements had to be made for passengers to pay for their travel and to board and alight from trains. On the Stockton & Darlington Railway, opened in 1825, no platforms were provided for passengers and they obtained their tickets at nearby inns. The Whitby & Pickering Railway opened about a decade later, and the history of Beckhole, one of the 'stopping places', illustrates various challenges that confront railway researchers. Even its name causes problems: Beck Hole, Beck Holes and Beckholes are other versions that have been seen.

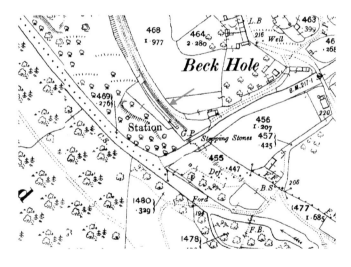

Whitby is a delightful coastal holiday resort and fishing harbour at the mouth of the River Esk. It is backed by the extensive and lofty North York Moors. Alec Clifton Taylor, in *Another Six English Towns* (1984), selected it as one of the most authentic Victorian towns, characterised by its densely packed cottages and steep streets, and dominated by the ruins of the abbey on the East Cliff. In the 18th century Whitby became a centre for shipbuilding and whaling as well as trading in alum and jet. Captain James Cook worked on vessels out of Whitby, and HMS *Endeavour*, the ship commanded by Cook on his voyage to Australia and New Zealand, was built in Whitby in 1764. Until the opening of the first turnpike road in 1759 Whitby relied on the sea for access, as the high plateau of the North York Moors formed a barrier between it and the rest of the country.

The Whitby & Pickering Railway (W&PR) was authorised by an Act of Parliament on 6 May 1833, and was a local initiative that was probably not conceived as part of a wider network; it also had no aspirations to embrace modern technology, as trains were to be horse-drawn. George Stephenson, a Northumbrian who had established his credentials as engineer to the Stockton & Darlington and Liverpool & Manchester railways, also had this role on the W&PR. The route he used followed the Esk valley from Whitby to Grosmont, one of the deep, narrow valleys that slice through the moors. At Grosmont there was a 144-yard tunnel, after which the route swung southward along the floor of the tributary valley of the Murk Esk to the hamlet of Beckhole. Immediately south was an incline, 1,500 yards in length, at an average gradient of 1 in 15, where horse traction gave way to rope-haulage. For much of the remainder of the route the line was built through the deep, winding Newtondale, and horse traction resumed from the top of the incline to the terminus at Pickering. The 520-foot summit of the route was in Newtondale at Fen Bog, where the marshy floor of the valley presented an engineering challenge and was crossed on a bed of timber and sheep fleeces. The line was to carry stone, timber and agricultural produce to Whitby for export, and passengers were to be conveyed too.

Tomlinson, in his *North Eastern Railway* (1914), notes that before the line was complete passenger traffic began to use the northern

Beckhole: This view, looking north, probably dates from the interwar years. The platform was in use in the summer only from 1908 until 1914. *John Mann and Martin Bairstow collections*

portion between Whitby and Grosmont from 8 June 1835, and by 18 July the W&PR announced that parties could charter trains to travel from Whitby as far as Beckhole. There was an isolated hamlet here, but the attractions were the nearby waterfalls of Mallyon Spout and Thomason Foss. The complete route opened formally on 26 May 1836, and an 1844 timetable shows two passenger services in each direction on weekdays between Whitby and Pickering. The combination of horse and rope traction made for a leisurely 2½-hour journey on the fastest train of the day.

On 7 July 1845 the York & North Midland Railway (Y&NMR) opened from York to Scarborough, with a branch from Rillington to Pickering; a week earlier this company had taken over the W&PR. No timetable evidence has been found of a station at Beckhole, although trains had to stop close to the hamlet at the foot of the incline where the rope or horse had to be attached for the train to continue its journey; it seems likely that local residents would have taken the opportunity to use the trains.

Reconstruction of the line as double track with heavier rails enabled steam locomotives to replace horses on the section between the foot of the incline and Whitby, and a locomotive shed was constructed at Beckhole to accommodate the engines. On the incline the original system, of using the weight of a water-filled tank on a northbound train to draw a southbound train uphill by rope, gave way to a stationary steam engine.

Beckhole: A North Eastern Railway steam 'autocar' stands at the station some time between 1908 and 1914. The 0-4-4 back tank engine is between two coaches that have been converted for push-pull working, with a driving compartment at each end of the train. *Martin Bairstow collection*

In 1854 the North Eastern Railway was formed by the amalgamation of several companies, including the Y&NMR. The NER was dissatisfied with the outmoded operation of the line, and by an Act of 11 July 1861 a 4½-mile deviation to avoid the incline was authorised from Grosmont to a point south of the village of Goathland, but even this route was steeply graded, mostly at 1 in 49. A station had served this village on the old route, and a new one (initially called Goathland Mill) replaced it on the deviation. The new line opened on 1 July 1865 and the old one was abandoned, except for the 2-mile section from Grosmont to Beckhole, which was retained to carry freight, particularly coal, to the isolated community. If it had been operating as an unadvertised passenger station, Beckhole would have closed at this stage. There was hope that the hamlet might prosper when an ironworks was built there; it began production in June 1861, but lasted less than 18 months.

Beckhole's status as a stopping place on the through route is uncertain, and it is possible that it had no platform or other facilities in this period. However, in a remarkable turn of events the NER decided to exploit the growing popularity of Whitby as a holiday resort by operating a summer-only 'autocar' train service in 1908 between the town and Beckhole for holidaymakers to enjoy a stroll and admire the waterfalls in their wooded valleys. The train service was repeated in 1909 and each summer until 1914. A conveniently dated OS plan of 1913 shows and names the station, which now had a short platform west of the single track and a timber building immediately south of the platform. The outbreak of war brought an end to the seasonal passenger train service, and it was never restored. However, the branch to Beckhole continued to carry freight until 1951, by which time road access to the hamlet had been improved. The OS 1-inch map of 1955 shows that the rails had been lifted. The trackbed is now used as a footpath, and nothing remains of the station.

The Whitby-Pickering-Malton route continued to carry passengers, but it was recommended for closure in the Beeching Report of March 1963 together with the two other routes serving Whitby. Although the Middlesbrough-Whitby 'Esk Valley' line was spared, the coastal route from Scarborough and the line to Pickering and Malton both closed on 8 March 1965. The section from Grosmont to Pickering closed to all traffic on that date, but Malton-Pickering continued to carry freight until 4 July 1966. The tracks of the entire route remained in place, and when in the summer of 1967 track-lifting was expected to begin, a railway preservation group expressed interest in operating trains for tourists at least on the Grosmont-Pickering section. Thanks to financial support from the North Riding County Council, the North York Moors National Park and the English Tourist Board, the route from Grosmont to Pickering reopened on 22 April 1973, and continues to thrive as the North Yorkshire Moors Railway; since 2003 advertised NYMR trains have run through to Whitby.

TOLLERTON (1841 & 1899)

First station	
Date opened	Probably with the line on 31 March 1841
Location	On East Coast Main Line between York and Darlington, several hundred yards north-east of Tollerton village where Station Road becomes Sykes Lane; immediately south-east of Sykes Lane bridge
Company on opening	Great North of England Railway
Date closed to passengers	1899
Date closed completely	1 November 1965
Company on closing to passenger services	North Eastern Railway
Company on closing to goods services	British Rail (North Eastern Region)
Present state	Demolished
County	Yorkshire North Riding (now North Yorkshire)
OS grid ref	SE516645

Second station	
Date opened	1899
Location	Immediately north-west of Sykes Lane bridge
Company on opening	North Eastern Railway
Date closed to passengers	1 November 1965
Date closed completely	1 November 1965
Company on closing	British Rail (North Eastern Region)
Present state	Demolished, but goods shed, cattle dock and stationmaster's house survive
County	Yorkshire North Riding (now North Yorkshire)
OS grid ref	SE515646

Until 1958 a journey through Yorkshire on the East Coast Main Line passed through 20 stations. Ten years later only five remained open. A purge of 13 minor stations took place in 1958-59, followed by Temple Hirst in 1961. Only one minor station, Tollerton, remained, and it did not escape the attention of the Beeching Report, in which its closure was recommended.

The section of the London King's Cross to Newcastle and Edinburgh main line between York and Darlington on which Tollerton station stood was built by the Great North of England Railway (GNoER). The project was envisaged by Joseph Pease, a prominent figure in the development of the Stockton & Darlington Railway (S&DR), who saw it as a means of connecting Tyneside and Darlington with the proposed York & North Midland Railway. By an Act of 12 July 1837 the York-Croft (Darlington) scheme was approved and the line opened to passengers on 31 March 1841; at the northern end it incorporated part of the S&DR's Croft branch.

At this point it is appropriate to introduce the 'Railway King', George Hudson, to the

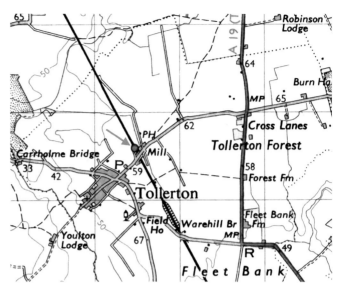

Tollerton: In this undated southward view from the up platform of the second station, the original station building can be seen immediately beyond the road bridge on the right, with the signal box beside it. *John Mann collection*

story. He was an ambitious man, active in the political life of Yorkshire and County Durham, and was involved in the promotion of many railways in Britain in the 1830s and '40s, principally in North East England and the Midlands. His enterprise and energy were matched by his ruthlessness and dishonesty, and his reputation collapsed in 1848-49. His favoured architect was George Townsend Andrews; many stations on lines associated with Hudson received Andrews's buildings, some

of great merit, and one of his smaller station buildings was found at Tollerton. (Several of Andrews's stations will be encountered in the early chapters of this book.)

The route from York as far as Eryholme

Tollerton: 'A4' 'Pacific' No 60007 *Sir Nigel Gresley* heads 'The Talisman' northwards on the down fast track, probably in the 1950s. *Jim Lake collection*

(about 40 miles) has negligible gradients, which has enabled it to carry some of Britain's fastest trains. The NER (successor in 1854 to the York, Newcastle & Berwick, previously the York & Newcastle, and the GNoER), together with the Great Northern and North British railways, entered into competition with the companies operating the West Coast route (London Euston-Carlisle–Edinburgh), and this encouraged the acceleration of services from the 1880s. The NER even had plans to electrify its main line, but the LNER (from 1923) took them no further. However, the famous Gresley-designed 'A4' 'Pacifics' of the later LNER and early BR years, the 'Deltic' (Class 55) diesels, and the InterCity 125 (Class 43) high-speed trains served the ECML until electrification of the route all the way from King's Cross to Edinburgh was accomplished in 1991, when Class 91 locomotives were introduced to haul the expresses.

Tollerton station was 9¾ miles north-west of York. It is likely to have opened with the line, but the earliest passenger timetables make no reference to it. The original site was immediately south of Sykes Lane crossing, about half a mile north-east of Tollerton village. The route was built as double track and there were two facing platforms. The station house and main passenger facilities were on the down (Darlington-bound) platform, towards its north-western end; in common with other stations

built or influenced by G. T. Andrews, there was a bay window on the platform elevation. Sidings were placed behind, and south-east, of the up platform, while the signal box was immediately north-west of the road crossing, on the down side of the tracks. The passenger service in the May 1849 timetable consisted of three departures in each direction on weekdays and two on Sunday. By 1863 the service had increased to four up and down departures and two Sunday trains in each direction.

In 1853 a branch opened from the main line at Pilmoor, north-west of Tollerton, to Gilling and Malton, the passenger services operating from Thirsk, also on the main line beyond Pilmoor. In 1871 a further branch opened, linking Gilling, Helmsley, Kirbymoorside and Pickering, and train services on this route ran from York, through Tollerton, and left the main line at Raskelf, two stations north of Tollerton. These trains generally called at Tollerton.

The heavily used main line suffered from congestion, and most of the York-Darlington section was quadrupled in stages over a period of almost 60 years. The first widening project was enabled by an Act of 1894, permitting the NER to quadruple from north of Beningbrough, through Tollerton, to a point south of Alne. This operation included the demolition of Tollerton station's platforms, south of Sykes Lane, and their replacement with a new (second) station immediately north-west of the road; the latter now crossed the line by a bridge. The new station had two platforms, with a wide gap between them as a result of being on the outer two tracks (the up and down slow lines). The

Tollerton: The up platform is photographed from a northbound express in 1961. The last advertised service to use this platform had been withdrawn by May 1959, and it looks distinctly neglected. Trains called at the down platform until the station closed in 1965. *Phil Reeks*

earlier station building survived, although it lost its bay to allow space for the down slow track. Construction of the new station was authorised in 1899, including a house for the stationmaster and a cottage. Somewhat modest buildings were

constructed on the platforms. These were small single-storey brick structures with a ridged roof and a small mock-Tudor central gable to add some weak, but fashionable, Arts and Crafts decoration. The sidings on the up side, beyond the road bridge, continued to be used, but an additional siding was provided as a bay set into the north-west end of the down platform. The signal box north-west of the road was replaced with one immediately south-east, again on the down side.

NER records show that in 1911 about 1,300 people were served by Tollerton station and that 10,740 tickets were issued: a small number for the days before motor bus competition emerged. In 1913 the station was handling coal, hay and clover, potatoes and livestock. A goods shed had been provided at the north-western end of the old sidings, at the foot of the road embankment, probably when the quadrupling took place.

Tollerton never enjoyed a frequent train service and, as elsewhere in Britain, competition from road motor transport was felt increasingly

Tollerton: After closure to passengers in 1965 a short section of the up platform was retained, seen here in August 1969. It was probably used as a 'staff halt' serving the adjacent engineer's yard. *John Mann*

*Above:***Tollerton:** The up 'Flying Scotsman' speeds past the site of the second station in March 2010. *John Furnevel*

Below: **Tollerton:** This is the site of the second station looking north-west in October 2014. *Nick Catford*

during the interwar years. In 1923 the NER became part of the LNER, and this company was prepared to discontinue unprofitable train services, as it demonstrated in North East England where several lines and many stations closed between 1929 and 1931. The minor stations between York and Darlington remained open; indeed, several were rebuilt in the 1930s when further sections of the route were quadrupled. However, by the winter of 1937-38 Tollerton's service had been reduced to five up and four down weekday trains and, significantly, there was no convenient provision made for local people returning from work in York. On Sunday there were two trains southbound to York, and two northbound, one to Newcastle and the other to Northallerton.

At nationalisation on 1 January 1948 Tollerton became part of BR's North Eastern Region. The station was no longer served by trains on Sunday – these had ceased by the summer of 1943 – and in the summer of 1952 the weekday service was minimal, with only two up and three down departures on Monday to Friday, and one more in each direction on Saturday. On 2 February 1953 the York-Helmsley-Pickering service ceased, leaving Tollerton with one morning train in each direction – 7.00am to Edinburgh and 7.49am to Doncaster – of no value whatever for an outward and return trip on the same day. By August 1959 Tollerton's train service was halved, leaving the one solitary northbound morning train, the primary purpose of which was probably the delivery of parcels. The TUCC report in July 1965 noted that in addition to the advertised northbound passenger train a southbound evening parcels train called at Tollerton.

The quaint and little-used station at Tollerton was joined in January 1961 by a new signal box of striking modern design, placed 300 yards south-east on the up side of the tracks. The box was part of a signalling upgrade of the main line following the completion of the

quadrupling projects in 1959, and controlled 12 route miles; it closed in 1989 when a facility at York took control of a much longer stretch of the route. By the 1960s Tollerton station was an antiquity, still lit by oil lanterns. Only the hand-painted running-in nameboards in dull tangerine BR(NE) livery were evidence that it might still be open. Despite its paltry train service the station continued to be staffed. It came as no surprise that the Beeching Report earmarked Tollerton for closure, but there was a considerable delay before the publication of the closure proposals on 13 March 1965. In the meantime a traffic survey revealed that in the week ending 11 July 1964 only one passenger joined a train and one alighted at Tollerton. A further survey in the week ending 24 October 1964 found that no passengers used the station.

The TUCC report presented to Tom Fraser, Minister of Transport, on 22 July 1965 noted that the only objection to closure by a user of Tollerton was from a Mr Slinger, who dispatched honey bees from the station. A Londoner objected to the closure (as well as to that of Gateshead West) on the grounds that if he sent in an objection an enquiry would have to be held; however, his complaint could not be considered as he was a week late in submitting it! On 19 August 1965 the Minister consented to the closure. A short time later, on 6 September, Tollerton ceased to handle goods traffic, and on 1 November 1965 the station closed to passengers, the final train having called on 30 October.

The platforms and buildings were soon demolished, but a very short section of platform, with ramps at each end, was left under the road bridge on the up side, possibly for use by staff working at the engineer's sidings in the former goods yard. Although the original station building, south of the road bridge, was demolished in 1988, the stationmaster's house, built with the second station, the goods shed, cattle dock and sidings to the south-east of the road bridge all survive.

CASTLE HOWARD (1845)

Date opened	8 July 1845
Location	On still-open York-Scarborough line, at end of unnamed lane
Company on opening	York & North Midland Railway
Date closed to passengers	22 September 1930
Date closed completely	2 November 1959
Company on closing to passenger services	London & North Eastern Railway
Company on closing to goods services	British Railways (North Eastern Region)
Present state	Platforms demolished, but station building survives
County	Yorkshire North Riding (now North Yorkshire)
OS grid ref	SE737667

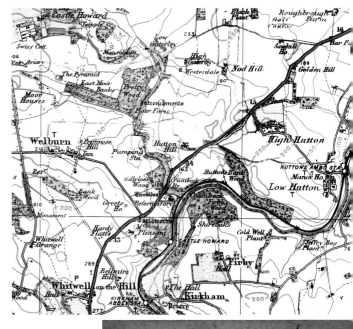

The 42-mile railway from York to Scarborough remains open and offers fascinating contrasts in scenery along its route. After leaving the built-up area of York the line follows a fairly direct route through farmland and stretches of lowland heath near Strensall, but after about 12 miles the railway joins the River Derwent in a tightly meandering route through Kirkham Abbey Gorge, before emerging onto the wide, flat floor of the Vale of Pickering and reaching Malton. Thereafter the line is almost level and nearly straight until it reaches Seamer, a few miles short of Scarborough. Of the 15 intermediate stations between York and Scarborough Central (16 after 1926), the majority served small rural settlements, with Malton the only town on the route. During the 1920s the development of motor bus services snatched much of the traffic formerly handled by the minor stations, and the bold decision was taken by the LNER in 1930 to withdraw passenger services from every

station between York and Scarborough apart from Malton, Seamer (the junction for lines to Pickering and Bridlington) and Scarborough's excursion station (Londesborough Road). By discontinuing the local stopping trains, more pathways were available for expresses that served Scarborough, where tourism expanded in the interwar years. Castle Howard station was one of the casualties (as was Rillington, which is the next station to be dealt with).

The York-Scarborough line was an important part of the network developed by the York & North Midland Railway (Y&NMR) headed by George Hudson. Although plans for this line were under way by 1839, it was not until 4 July 1844 that the Act was passed authorising its construction, and it opened a year later on 8 July 1845. Until 1877, when the present station opened, trains from Scarborough had to reverse at York North Junction to enter the York terminus.

Castle Howard station opened with the line, although it did not appear in timetables until mid-1848. The station was in the scenic gorge where the line meanders through the Howardian Hills. The route was originally planned to have a 1,430-yard tunnel through the hills, but the cheaper option of hugging

Castle Howard: This undated photograph is looking south from the up platform. The contrast between the timber waiting rooms to the left and the stately main building on the opposite platform is striking. *John Mann collection*

the river bank added 1¾ miles to the line and required a 40mph restriction for the 3¾-mile-long series of bends. The station's potential traffic was limited by its riverside position, with no crossing over the Derwent, and only isolated farmsteads and cottages and the village of Welburn (1¼ miles away) within reasonable walking distance. The stately home of Castle Howard was more than 2½ miles to the north-west. Only three-quarters of a mile separated Castle Howard station from Kirkham Abbey,

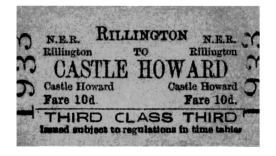

N.E.R. **RILLINGTON** N.E.R.
Rillington   TO   Rillington
CASTLE HOWARD
Castle Howard   Castle Howard
Fare 10d.   **Fare 10d.**
THIRD CLASS THIRD
Issued subject to regulations in time tables

the next stop en route to York. In 1911 only 6,601 tickets were booked.

As it served the stately home of the Earls of Carlisle, Castle Howard station was provided with a fine building by G. T. Andrews, who also designed the original station at Tollerton and several others featured in this volume. Although open to the public, the station was essentially for the convenience of the Earl, his family and guests, and he was permitted to stop trains on request by displaying a flag or signal. The entrance to the two-storey station house was through an arched porch, above which was a room with an arched window with blind panels on either side. Although resembling other stations by this architect, it had an enlarged single-storey office range with a series of arched window openings and, as Fawcett (2001) puts it, a rather theatrical balcony, embodying the popular Venetian window motif and boldly corbelled out above the platform. An elaborate Italianate gable finial added interest to the balcony. The attractive building, constructed of

Castle Howard: A general view looking north in the 1930s. The handsome building on the left, a design by G. T. Andrews, was thought fitting for use by the Earls of Carlisle after whose residence the station was named. *John Mann collection*

local Hildenley Quarry limestone, was finished off with generous roof projections and two groups of robust chimney stacks. In contrast to the elaborate building on the down platform, the facing up platform had only a timber pent-roof enclosed waiting shelter, and a signal box stood at its southern end.

Goods facilities were immediately south of the passenger station on the down (Scarborough-bound) side, consisting of a single siding entered from the north, with a 5-ton crane and facilities to handle the normal range of traffic such as furniture vans, livestock and horse boxes. In 1913 NER records show that barley, hay/clover and livestock were dealt with at Castle Howard. The signal box controlled a down relief siding; stopping trains were reversed into this to permit expresses to pass.

Early in its life the station was used by Queen Victoria in August 1850 when she was entertained by the Earl at Castle Howard on her way to open Newcastle Central station and the Royal Border Bridge. A contemporary illustration shows that a porch was provided on the platform in front of the waiting rooms for the comfort of the distinguished visitor.

Bradshaw of February 1863 indicates a weekday service of two up departures, with two more by request, and one on Sunday; in the

Castle Howard: A southbound DMU excursion calls at the station on 24 August 1961. *A. L. Barnett, NERA*

opposite direction there were four departures, plus one by request, and one on Sunday. In July 1896 the service had improved to five up departures on weekdays (three on Sunday) and seven down departures (two on Sunday). In

Castle Howard: By June 1978 both platforms had been demolished but the station building was in residential use, as it still is. *Alan Young*

June 1920 the NER provided five up and six down departures on weekdays, and one Sunday train in each direction.

As noted earlier, competition from road transport was so serious that Castle Howard and the other wayside stations between York and Scarborough closed to passengers in 1930. However, the station remained intact and goods traffic continued to be handled until 2 November 1959. For some time the waiting room on the up platform was converted into a camping cottage and let to holidaymakers in the same way that camping coaches were used. Excursions occasionally called at the closed stations, and one such visit to Castle Howard was by a DMU on 24 August 1961.

The platforms are understood to have been demolished in the 1960s, but not only can Castle Howard's station building still be admired from passing trains, but also those at many other stations that closed with it on the York–Scarborough line; Huttons Ambo, the next station on the way to Malton, is particularly attractive.

RILLINGTON (1845)

Date opened	8 July 1845
Location	On still-open York-Scarborough line, immediately north-east of level crossing on Low Moor Lane
Company on opening	York & North Midland Railway
Date closed to passengers	22 September 1930
Date closed completely	10 August 1964
Company on closing to passenger services	London & North Eastern Railway
Company on closing to goods services	British Railways (North Eastern Region)
Present state	Station building in residential use
County	Yorkshire East Riding (now North Yorkshire)
OS grid ref	SE844753

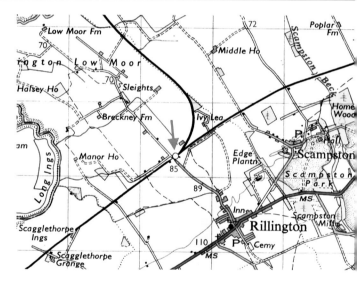

It must have been a remarkable experience in the early 1950s when travelling by train between York and Scarborough to have passed through Rillington station. Set amidst fields and three-quarters of a mile from the small village after which it was named, here was a station fit for a town, complete with an overall roof – yet it had been closed since 1930.

Rillington station was a near neighbour of Castle Howard, also on the York to Scarborough line. It was immediately west of the point where the branch to Pickering left the York-Scarborough route, both lines having opened on 8 July 1845. At Pickering this branch connected with an existing line to provide a through route to Whitby (as described in the Beckhole entry above). In the expectation that it would be the interchange point between the 'main line' and the Pickering route, Rillington station was provided with an overall roof, or 'trainshed', for passenger comfort. However, in practice passengers to and from Pickering would have changed trains at Malton, the next station towards York, so the lavish provision at Rillington was not really needed. The station was called 'Rillington Junction' in Bradshaw until the mid-1890s.

The main building at Rillington was another by G. T. Andrews, but less ambitious than that at Castle Howard. Standing on the south-east (up) side of the tracks, it was a brick-built two-storey structure with a pair of ground-floor canted bay windows facing the platform on either side of an arched doorcase. While in most of Andrews's stations the building was aligned at right angles to the railway track, at Rillington it was placed parallel to the platform. The slated hipped-roof trainshed was typical

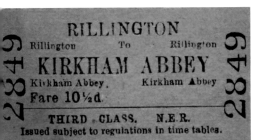

of those designed by Andrews, covering the platform frontage of the building and supported on the opposite platform by a tall screen wall. Goods facilities were on the up side, immediately north-east of the passenger station, consisting of three sidings, one of which served a coal depot behind the up platform. The normal range of goods was handled, and in 1913 barley and livestock were the principal traffic.

In February 1863 the Bradshaw timetable noted that passengers for Pickering and Whitby were to change at Malton, and that three up trains to York and four to Scarborough called at Rillington only 'when passengers are booked

Rillington: Looking north-east from the level crossing circa 1910, the down platform (left) is backed by the wall supporting the trainshed, while the main building is out of sight on the up platform. In the distance the splitting signal controls the junction ahead where the Pickering and Whitby route leaves the main line to Scarborough. *Alan Young collection*

there'; in each direction only one Monday-to-Friday and two Saturday trains in each direction made an unconditional call at Rillington. On Sunday one 'main-line' train called in each direction and there was one Pickering branch departure and arrival. In June 1920 eight weekday up trains called at Rillington, four each from Scarborough and Whitby, and there was one Sunday call from Scarborough; the down timetable had the same frequencies.

As noted in the Castle Howard entry above, by the 1920s most of the intermediate stations between York and Scarborough booked very few passengers. According to NER 1911 statistics, Rillington served a population of 1,164 and issued 12,796 tickets, but bus services, which grew in frequency after the First World War, enticed passengers from the railway. Rillington and the other four minor stations between Malton and Seamer were inconveniently sited to serve the nearest villages, and they closed in September 1930, as did all stations between York and Malton.

Above: **Rillington:** Looking south-west in 1955, Class 4MT 2-6-4 No 80118 is heading a train for Whitby. The trainshed is still in place, but was to be demolished within a few months. *Alan Brown collection*

Below: **Rillington:** Probably in the early 1950s Class 'D49' 4-4-0 No 62726 *The Meynell* hurries through the deserted station with a train from Scarborough. The trainshed remained in place for 25 years after the station closed to passengers, latterly stripped of its cladding. *Alan Brown collection*

After its official closure Rillington was used by passengers on Saturdays from 4 July to 10 October 1942, and again from 2 October 1944 possibly until 1 October 1945, but these calls were not shown in the public timetable. Goods services continued until 10 October 1964. The overall roof covered the former passenger platforms and track until 1955, but it latterly retained only the ironwork as the slates had been removed. The station building survives today somewhat altered, and the distinctive bay windows have been removed from the platform elevation.

Top: **Rillington:** Looking east circa 1971, the two bay windows of the station building, characteristic of the Y&NMR buildings designed by G.T. Andrews, will be noted. *John Mann collection*

Centre: **Rillington:** The station building and signal box are seen from a passing train in April 1974. A fragment of the up platform remains in place. *Alan Young*

Right: **Rillington:** This is the station building, looking east in October 2008. The bay windows have been removed from the platform elevation. *John Furnevel*

RICHMOND (1846)

Date opened	10 September 1846
Location	Station Yard, off Station Road (A6136)
Company on opening	York & Newcastle Railway
Date closed to passengers	3 March 1969
Date closed completely	3 March 1969
Company on closing	British Rail (Eastern Region)
Present state	Grade II* building has been restored as a leisure facility, and the engine shed, gasworks, stationmaster's house and railway cottages also survive
County	Yorkshire North Riding (now North Yorkshire)
OS grid ref	NZ176008

Richmond is a small market town (population about 8,200) on the River Swale. Both the town and upper Swaledale have great charm; indeed, the architectural historian Alec Clifton Taylor selected Richmond as one of his favourites in the BBC television series *Six English Towns* in 1978, and the writer and fell-walker Alfred Wainwright considered Swaledale the finest of the Yorkshire Dales. Richmond's name was transplanted from the town of Richemont in Normandy. The castle on its cliff overlooking the rock-strewn River Swale was completed in 1086, and still guards a bridge over the river.

The town centre remains quaint and bustling, with its large, cobbled market place and the old Trinity church at the centre. Upstream of Richmond, Swaledale produced wool and lead, and Richmond, the local market town, benefited from the prosperity of the lead

Richmond: The frontage of the station is seen in 1951, looking south-east across the forecourt. The flamboyant architecture of medieval appearance with a heavily buttressed Gothic entrance arcade is the work of G. T. Andrews. The stone-built goods shed is in the background. *John Mann collection*

industry, as testified by its wealth of Georgian buildings.

The railway reached Richmond in 1846. It was the terminus of a double-track branch from what is now the East Coast Main Line, whose history has already been described in the Tollerton entry above. The incentive to serve Richmond was principally the promise of mineral traffic, as the railhead for Swaledale lead had been the Stockton & Darlington Railway's Croft Depot near Darlington (from 1829), then, from its opening in 1841, Cowton on the York-Darlington main line. To reach these transhipment points, horses had to negotiate uneven roads and trackways. The Richmond branch, 9 miles 62 chains long, left the main line at Dalton Junction, six miles south of Darlington, and stations were provided at the junction – later renamed Eryholme – and at Moulton, Scorton and Catterick Bridge. Only the terminus at Richmond offered much prospect of passenger traffic as well as the

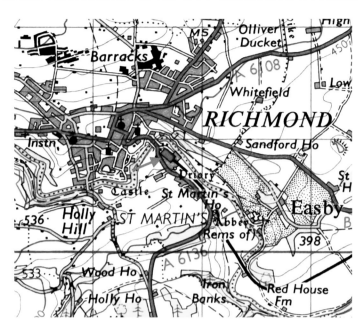

lead for which the branch was intended, and the general goods that would be expected of a market town.

Although the villages and the lead mines of upper Swaledale could have provided traffic, the railway never advanced beyond Richmond. The Reeth & Richmond Railway was authorised in 1869, but nothing came of the scheme. In 1912 North Riding County Council was willing to support a projected light railway into upper Swaledale, and the Treasury promised a £17,000 loan, but the scheme was eventually talked out, largely on account of the heavy demands made

by the NER for the use of Richmond station and for working the line.

Richmond was favoured with a fine station. Fawcett (2011) considers that there is nothing else quite like it among British stations and that it is 'one of the most evocative stations of the early Railway Age – a Romantic response to a highly picturesque setting'. G. T. Andrews, whom we have already encountered, designed the station, and he appears to have ignored the instructions of the Chairman of the Great North Eastern Railway – the company that had obtained the Act for the Richmond branch – for the station to be inexpensive. Because construction had barely begun when the railway opened in September 1846, a temporary wooden passenger shed sufficed until April 1847.

The permanent terminus was in local sandstone, of almost medieval appearance with a heavily buttressed Gothic entrance arcade of five pointed arches on the north-east elevation, fronting a tall office range. Slightly lower, the flanking building was lit by tall mullioned windows, including a gabled bay. The roofs were steeply pitched, and there was a series of tall, paired chimney stacks. This building abutted the single platform and originally contained (from south-east to north-west) a walled yard, gents' toilet, waiting room, then – possibly – the stationmaster's office, followed by the booking office. Beyond the

Richmond: The north-west end of the station under the trainshed is seen in 1952. The structure of the roofing can be seen, with one pitched roof above the platform and its single track, separated by an elegant arcade from the goods sidings under the other pitched roof. The station was frequently used by military personnel travelling to or from Catterick Camp – as seen in this photographand on the 'furlough' ticket (page 27). *John Mann collection*

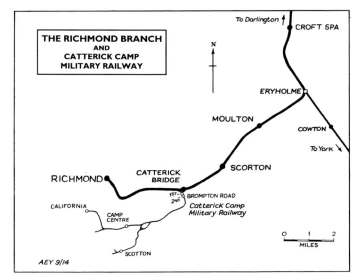

Richmond: A map of the Richmond and Catterick Camp branches. *Alan Young*

entrance were a refreshment room, kitchen, 1st Class waiting room, and finally the ladies' waiting room-cum-toilet. The platform line was accompanied by two sidings, often used to hold horse boxes hired out to local trainers for racehorses. All three lines were covered by a trainshed of great distinction, which consisted of twin 30-foot-wide pitched roofs, one sheltering the platform and adjacent line, and the other covering the two sidings; an

arcade with slender octagonal columns and elaborately decorated spandrels, between the platform line and the two sidings, supported the roofs. At the north-western end the twin pitched roofs had a double-gabled 'screen' to complement the front elevation, complete with buttresses, and windows at ground and upper levels, one of the ground floor windows having a gabled bay. The open end of the trainshed was striking in appearance. The steeply pitched twin

Richmond: Passengers, sharing the platform with assorted parcel trolleys, wait for the DMU that is approaching the station circa 1963. BR(NE) signage accompanies the LNER electric lighting. The terrace of six railway cottages and the signal box can be seen in the distance. *Ken Hoole collection/NERA*

gables were of timber, with a pair of mullioned windows in each. The planks of the gables were arranged in herringbone fashion, and the plain-edged bargeboards carried intricate details and a finial-cum-pendant. A similar bargeboard and finial graced the end of the trainshed-ridge skylights. It is a pleasure to note that, apart from the platform, these buildings survive.

The passenger station was accompanied by a range of other facilities that included a goods shed and a two-road engine shed, with one line continuing beyond it to a coal depot, a 45-foot turntable, a gas works, a water pumping station, a 3-ton crane, and a signal box of early NER (Southern Division) design. A stationmaster's house of restrained Gothic design was provided south-west of the passenger facilities. Further accommodation was provided in six general staff cottages, two further cottages for goods staff, and a goods agent's house.

At first the low, single platform extended only a short distance beyond the trainshed, but it was lengthened in 1860 and raised at its front edge, sloping

Richmond: Possibly in 1963 a Metro-Cammell DMU waits under the trainshed. The distinctive gable ends of the twin trainshed roofs, with the timber planks arranged in a herringbone pattern and with patterned bargeboards, can be enjoyed in this view. *Ken Hoole collection/ NERA*

Richmond: In November 1972 the station has been closed for more than three years and the rails have been removed, although the LNER lamp standards remain in place. The stationmaster's house is visible to the left of the station building, and the goods shed is to the right. *John Mann*

Richmond: The station building and trainshed are in use as 'Richmond Garden & Farm Supply Centre' in August 1978. *Alan Young*

down to the original platform level to provide safe access to the offices. Further lengthening was carried out in 1892, and again in 1915 to accommodate military traffic, by which time it reached 268 yards. During the First World War there was a rearrangement of offices and waiting rooms, and at about the same time the large window at the terminal end was opened up to provide a large door for handling parcels. Despite these improvements to the facilities, a

second platform, for which space was provided under the south-west roof of the trainshed, was never built.

The original passenger service consisted of three trains each way between Darlington and Richmond; a fourth was added by the end of 1846, together with three trains on Sunday. In the early days some branch trains terminated at Dalton. By 1870 there were five weekday branch trains, and seven in 1896. Richmond

Above: **Richmond:** The trainshed is seen again in August 1978 from a similar viewpoint to one of the photographs taken about 15 years earlier. The foreground has been landscaped as part of the garden centre that occupies the trainshed. *Alan Young*

Right: **Richmond:** Now a popular leisure and commercial enterprise known as 'The Station', the architecture has been sensitively preserved, as seen in November 2009. *Alan Young*

branch trains generally called at Croft Spa, on the main line just north of the border between County Durham and Yorkshire; this station is featured in the companion volume *Lost stations of Northumberland & Durham.* The annual Whit Monday Athletic Sports and Bicycle Meet attracted excursions to Richmond from Middlesbrough, Saltburn and Bishop Auckland and additional trains from Darlington.

The First World War had major implications for the Richmond branch. In 1908 Lord Baden Powell had proposed that a military camp should be provided in the locality, and in 1914, after the outbreak of war, work began on an extensive site south of Richmond. Catterick Camp's first troops arrived in 1916, and the facility was served by a railway that branched

from the Richmond line at Catterick Bridge; at one time it had four stations and carried military passengers and goods traffic. Richmond station was also used by service personnel travelling to and from the camp, which remained in use after hostilities ended and is today known as Catterick Garrison.

On 1 May 1933 Sentinel steam railcars were introduced on the Richmond branch, but by 1937 they had been largely withdrawn and limited to Sundays. The winter 1937-38 timetable shows 11 weekday departures and nine on Sunday from Richmond, and the same frequency applied in June 1943 during the Second World War. In early BR days the frequency of advertised passenger services increased, with 13 weekday and nine Sunday

Richmond: In November 2009 a restaurant occupies the heart of the former trainshed. The columns that support the two pitched roofs and divided the passenger and goods areas can be seen, now painted red, in the middle of the dining area. *Alan Young*

departures from Richmond in the summer of 1952. However, troop trains were less numerous, and by the late 1950s there was only a Friday afternoon departure for Newcastle, a Saturday lunchtime departure for London, and three early-morning trains returning to the camp from Darlington. The summer 1959 public timetable's only evidence of military needs was the 12.30am Monday-only departure from Darlington, arriving at Richmond at 12.58. On 19 August 1957 diesel multiple units replaced steam on routine Richmond branch services, and in the late 1950s they operated about a dozen return workings on weekdays, with a similar number on summer Sundays, but only two or three on Sundays during the winter.

Maps in the Beeching Report indicated that the Richmond branch carried fewer than 5,000 passengers per week – the lowest category. At that time there were still 11 Monday-Friday departures from Richmond, with 12 on Saturday and two on Sunday. The line was earmarked for closure and formal notice was published on 11 October 1963. However, on 30 December 1964 Tom Fraser, Secretary of State for Transport, refused permission for closure. The military branch had already closed to passengers on 26 October 1964, and saw its last steam working when visited by 'Three Dales Railtour' on 20 May 1967.

Few economies had been exercised by

British Railways in operating the Richmond branch, although Moulton was demoted to an unstaffed halt on 1 October 1956 and, apart from the introduction of the DMUs in 1957, there was little evidence of modernisation. After the Second World War the LNER replaced gas lighting with electric at Richmond, and installed new nameplates, and BR fitted tangerine totem nameplates at Croft Spa and Scorton. However, in the mid-1960s BR singled the branch from a point 246 yards west of Catterick Bridge into Richmond, working the section under 'one engine in steam' and closing it to goods traffic from 2 October 1967. Redundant track and sidings were soon recovered, and Richmond's signal box and water column were demolished in August 1968. Proposals to close the branch were published for a second time on 26 January 1968, but this time the Secretary of State (Richard Marsh) consented on 11 November, and closure was effected on 3 March 1969. Until 9 February 1970 goods traffic continued on the branch as far as Catterick Bridge, but track-lifting began in February 1970 and was complete by October of that year.

Before it closed Richmond station received listed status, but it stood derelict until the District Council acquired the whole site. Although the goods shed was demolished, a remarkable assemblage of structures was preserved. By 1978 the station trainshed was used as a garden centre. However, this business closed in 2001, and two years later a community-based regeneration programme was approved, led by Richmondshire Building Preservation Trust. The outcome was a splendid leisure and commercial complex known, accurately if unimaginatively, as 'The Station'. It houses a restaurant and café bar, two cinema screens, a heritage centre, an art gallery, rooms for public use, and a range of artisan food producers, and there is an exhibition on the history of the branch. 300,000 visitors pass through its doors each year. The former engine shed has been restored as a fitness centre, and the site of the goods shed is occupied by a swimming pool. The site of the former coal depot is now a car park. The station building and trainshed, the heart of the complex, have been sensitively restored, making this one of the finest disused stations in Britain.

ERYHOLME (1846)

Date opened	10 September 1846
Location	On East Coast Main Line and former Richmond branch, half a mile north-west of B1263; a private track runs along the west side of the main line
Company on opening	York & Newcastle Railway
Date closed to passengers	1 October 1911
Date closed completely	Probably 3 March 1969
Company on closing to passengers	North Eastern Railway
Company on closing completely	British Rail (Eastern Region)
Present state	Some sections of prefabricated platform survive; other sections lie in a heap. Stone blocks from the platform building can be seen at ground level. Railway cottages and station building have been demolished.
County	Yorkshire North Riding (now North Yorkshire)
OS grid ref	NZ303060

This station was built to enable passengers to change between main-line and Richmond branch trains rather than to serve the locality. It is notable for its early disappearance from railway timetables but its survival for almost five decades with intermittent unadvertised use.

Although the York-Darlington section of the Great North of England Railway's line had opened in 1841, the station at Dalton Junction (later Eryholme) did not open until 1846, with the Richmond branch, and was situated at the point where the branch swung away from the main line. It stood in sparsely populated countryside without road access, taking its name from Dalton-on-Tees, a village some 2 miles north, whose parish included the station. Bradshaw ceased to include 'Junction' in the station name after 1893-94. Perhaps because of confusion with Dalton and Dalston on the coastal route between Carnforth and Carlisle, the NER altered the name on 1 July 1901 to Eryholme; this hamlet was even further

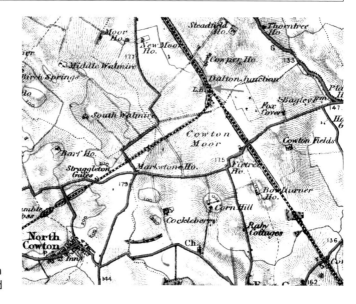

from the station than Dalton-on-Tees, but the NER had no qualms about naming stations after distant communities to avoid repeating station names.

Platforms were provided on the main line, connected by a typical arched NER footbridge. At its north-western end the down platform merged with the Richmond-bound

Eryholme: On 7 February 1953 'A5' No 69835 is hauling a passenger train past the long-closed station, whose main building is on the right; this is yet another of G. T. Andrews's designs. The platform is still in place at this time as certain trains continued to call for the benefit of railway staff and their families who lived in this somewhat remote location. *Alan Brown collection*

platform, while a short timber platform served passengers leaving trains from Richmond who intended to catch a southbound main-line train; they were carefully led across both Richmond tracks, then they used the footbridge to reach the up main-line platform. The station building was aligned with the main line on the down platform, but was placed to serve the Richmond platform too. The station house was a robust, stone-built T-shaped building, of Gothic character with decorated bargeboards, finials and tall chimneystacks. It was adjoined on the north-west side by a single-storey office range set at right-angles to the main line; a canted bay window on the main-line elevation was a typical G. T. Andrews feature. An unusual architectural feature was the large, open-sided waiting shed that continued north-west from the station house and office range. Fawcett (2011) notes that the shed was some 20 feet deep and 50 feet long, with a tall gabled roof carried on intermediate columns, ending with a pair of stone piers with buttresses splayed out diagonally, and he suggests that Andrews was probably inspired by the style of small Tudor market halls. On the up main-line platform a small timber shelter sufficed. The original signal box was at the north-west end of the up platform, but this was replaced on 1 June 1939 with a box at the north-west end of the combined down main-line and Richmond-line platform.

The May 1849 timetable showed one weekday and two Sunday main-line departures from Dalton Junction in each direction, with four weekday and three Sunday trains each way

on the Richmond branch. In February 1863 there were three weekday and two Sunday main-line departures for Darlington and four weekday and two Sunday trains to York, while five weekday and two Sunday trains called to and from Richmond. Ludlam (1993) notes that it was normal for branch trains to terminate at Dalton Junction. Renamed 'Eryholme', in April 1910 four weekday trains called in each direction at the main-line platforms, with two Sunday trains to Darlington and one to York. Four trains to Richmond (together with one by request) called on weekdays, with two on Sunday, and in the opposite direction there were five on weekdays (as well as one on Monday, by request) and two on Sunday.

On 1 October 1911 Eryholme closed to passengers, causing little inconvenience as connections between main-line and Richmond trains could be made at Croft Spa. Although no longer in the public timetable, trains continued to call at Eryholme for railway workers and their families who lived in the adjacent station cottages, and goods were still handled. Quick (2009) notes that LNER working timetables show Monday, Thursday, Friday and Saturday stops at Eryholme for railwaymen by Richmond branch trains. The up main-line platform was demolished shortly after closure, and the large waiting shed on the opposite and Richmond

Eryholme: This view from 1959 is looking south across the East Coast Main Line, and the Richmond branch can be seen curving sharply away. The station building is placed to serve both the down main-line and Richmond-bound platforms. The signal box seen here was built in 1939. Although main-line trains are not known to have called at the surviving platform, Richmond branch trains still made non-timetabled calls for railway staff and their families. *Stations UK*

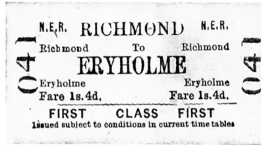

platforms probably disappeared at about the same time.

During the Second World War Eryholme had a new lease of life as a stopping place for RAF Croft, about a mile to the west; the NER Emergency Board authorised this on 17 February 1944. The Richmond-bound branch platform was extended south-westwards using prefabricated concrete panels, and a second platform was built for northbound trains. The winter 1945-46 working timetable shows additional calls for RAF personnel only. Unadvertised trains continued into BR days, working timetables issued in June and September 1961 showing stops in both directions for railwaymen and families on all days except Sundays. The author recalls that on Friday 15 May 1964 the 9.17am ex-Darlington stopped at Eryholme to take on passengers. On 1 June 1964 the station closed for goods traffic, though it is likely that none had been

handled for some time. The station building was demolished in the early 1960s. Unadvertised use of the station possibly continued until Darlington-Richmond passenger services were withdrawn on 3 March 1969. The branch tracks were removed in October 1970. The signal box closed on 31 January 1977 and was demolished in the 1980s. Today some fragments of the wartime branch platforms are all that remain.

Eryholme: Shortly before the end of the Second World War platforms of prefabricated concrete panels were added on the Richmond branch to serve personnel visiting or working at RAF Croft, and a new footbridge connected them. This is what remained of the platforms in September 2009. *Nick Catford*

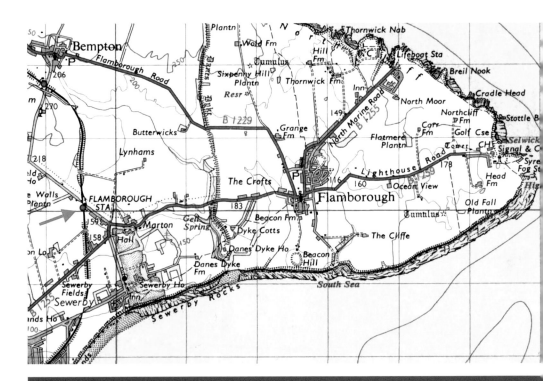

FLAMBOROUGH (1847)

Date opened	Probably with the line on 20 October 1847
Location	On still-open Hull-Scarborough line; south of level crossing on Jewison Lane
Company on opening	York & North Midland Railway
Date closed to passengers	5 January 1970
Date closed completely	5 January 1970
Company on closing	British Rail (Eastern Region)
Present state	Station building in residential use
County	Yorkshire East Riding (now North Yorkshire)
OS grid ref	TA195700

Another York & North Midland Railway route was the line that still connects Hull, Beverley, Driffield, Bridlington, Filey and Scarborough. The first section to open was Hull-Bridlington on 7 October 1846, followed by the line from Seamer (connecting with the York-Scarborough line) to Filey on 26 October 1846. The Bridlington-Filey gap was filled on 20 October 1847, completing a double-track route of almost 54 miles. From Hull to Bridlington the line passes through the almost flat terrain of Holderness, with numerous level

crossings, so 'the engineering requirements of the line could not have been more modest' (Addyman et al, 2013). North of Bridlington th Yorkshire Wolds, a broad chalk escarpment, reaches the coast, ending in the spectacular

Flamborough Head cliffs. Although the Wolds rise to less than 400 feet where the railway was to cross them, the chalk is hard and the need to excavate cuttings between Bridlington and Hunmanby – in addition to sluggishness in the completion of land purchases – delayed the opening of the Bridlington-Filey section on which Flamborough station was located. Serving Flamborough village was not a priority, and the line would have had to pursue a most indirect course to do so. The station was therefore 2 miles west of the village, much closer to Marton, a hamlet less than half a mile away and the name the station carried until 1 July 1884. Exactly when the station opened is not certain, as the earliest timetables did not include it – a frustrating situation for historians seeking opening dates for many stations in North East England.

G. T. Andrews designed a dignified station building placed immediately south of the level crossing on the up platform. The two-storey building is of local yellow brick under a hipped roof, and tall pilasters on both the west and north elevations have stone detailing in their capitals and bases, with sandstone used for window sills and architraves. Fawcett (2011) draws attention to the brick eaves cornice and the restrained portico in front of the booking office on the north elevation, which was demolished after the station closed. The extra effort made with Flamborough's building was to

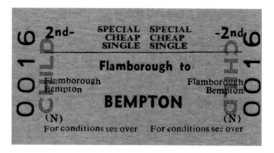

satisfy the Yarburgh family of nearby Sewerby Hall rather than visitors to Flamborough Head. The building received later extensions. Facing the main building was a long, enclosed pent-roofed timber shelter on the down platform.

From the 1870s, in summer months access from Flamborough village to its station was improved by a horse omnibus service. A project of 1887 to construct a 3½-mile 3-foot-gauge 'Flamborough Head Steam Tramways' from the station to the village and on to North Landing was abandoned. A further proposal in the late 1890s for a standard-gauge, possibly electrically operated, Flamborough & Bridlington Light

Flamborough: On 25 April 1957 Class 'D49' 4-4-0 No 62717 *Banffshire* draws a southbound train into the station. The main building is on the right, with an NER timber waiting shed on the opposite platform. The station is oil-lit and BR totem signs have been installed. *Les Turnbull*

Flamborough: The station is seen in September 1960, looking south-east. This is the sixth successive station in this survey to have a G. T. Andrews-designed building, with a dignity befitting the aristocratic Yarburgh family of Sewerby Hall: they and their guests would be numbered among the passengers. *G. C. Lewthwaite*

Railway also came to nothing. The NER showed interest in this project, but prior to the First World War provided its own summer bus service to Flamborough Head from Filey and Bridlington. It is interesting to note that the NER was an early provider of motor bus services instead of extending its railway network when in 1903 it abandoned plans for a 12½-mile branch railway from Beverley to North Frodingham and provided a 'Motor Car' (i.e. bus) service instead – too late to remove the phantom railway route from the tile maps that it installed at a number of principal stations.

In February 1863 Flamborough had three trains in each direction on weekdays and one on Sunday. In July 1896 the Sunday service was unchanged, but weekday departures had increased to eight. The LNER winter 1937-38 timetable showed seven northbound and five southbound departures, and one on Sunday.

In terms of its train service Flamborough was in the middle rank on the Hull-Scarborough line, with some neighbours such as Carnaby, Gristhorpe and Cayton having a markedly poorer service by the 1930s.

Fishing was the mainstay of Flamborough's economy. Small 'cobles' brought cod, crabs and lobsters ashore at the North and South Landing beaches, and some was dispatched by rail via the fish dock in the station's goods yard; fish wagons were allowed to run by gravity onto the rear of slow Scarborough-Hull trains when they were standing at the up platform. Cattle and coal were also handled in the yard, which was north of the level crossing on the up side of the line. North of the goods yard the railway passed through a rock cutting that was enlarged in 1876 to create a ballast quarry, and sidings were laid on either side of the running lines until the First World War. Addyman (2013) notes that although Flamborough was not one of the Hull-Scarborough line's most profitable stations, the NER recorded receipts that were three to four times the cost of its staff of three and that passenger income peaked in 1921 but had halved by the 1930s. In 1911 the station issued 10,618 tickets. During the First World War, as an economy measure, one of the tracks between Flamborough and Hunmanby was

Flamborough: The up platform and building are seen from a southbound train in April 1974. *Alan Young*

removed, probably for use in a munitions siding; double track was restored in 1923.

Under BR(NE) in the summer of 1950 Flamborough enjoyed six trains in each direction on weekdays (with one extra northbound on Saturday) and two Sunday trains each way. This frequency was maintained, with few changes, for the following two decades. In the early 1950s a modicum of modernisation occurred as BR totem name signs and running-in nameboards were installed, although these were still accompanied by oil lighting. This combination of totems and oil lamps was unusual in the NE Region, but was also found at Hunmanby and Bempton on the same line.

The Hull-Scarborough line was not recommended for closure by Beeching, although services were to be 'modified' and several stations were to close – Speeton, Carnaby, Burton Agnes, Lowthorpe and Arram – but not Flamborough. However, the lines through Market Weighton that joined the Hull-Scarborough route at Beverley and Driffield were on the closure list. The Selby-Driffield service ceased on 14 June 1965, followed by Hull-Beverley-York trains on 29 November

1965. A knock-on effect of the latter closure was that average passenger figures on the Hull-Scarborough route fell to below 50,000 per week, and in September 1966 it was identified as a candidate for closure. BR claimed that annual earnings were £366,400 against costs of £407,600. Inconclusive discussions were held with local authorities to establish whether they were prepared to make a financial contribution to the train service.

In January 1967 BR's North Eastern Region was merged with the Eastern. It is possible that the departure of Arthur Dean, the 'pro-closure' General Manager, and the extension of the remit of the Eastern Region's enterprising new General Manager, Gerald Fiennes, to include North East England, benefited the Hull-Scarborough route. He arranged an inspection of the line and recommended a number of economies, but almost simultaneously the 'Network for Development' map of March 1967 indicated that the Hull-Scarborough route should be closed to passengers and carry only freight as far north as Bridlington and close entirely through Flamborough and Filey to Seamer. On 3 April 1968 formal notice of closure was published with a view to enacting this on 7 October. However, the proposal drew a huge response of 3,444

Flamborough: Both the platform and the building are still in place in April 2004. *Alan Young*

written objections, the largest number that had ever been received opposing a closure. On 22 November 1968 a public hearing took place in Bridlington, where the main contentions were the increased journey times by bus on the inadequate road system – an extra 1 hour 43 minutes for a round trip between Filey and Hull; the loss of visitors to towns heavily dependent on holiday trade; and inevitable road congestion in summer. The TUCC reported that considerable hardship would be caused by closure, although the effects would be minimal on communities served by some minor stations, including Flamborough. On 29 July 1969 Richard Marsh, Secretary of State for Transport, consented only to the closure of certain stations, and Flamborough – not listed by Beeching – was one of them. A BR survey showed that on most days only one passenger

boarded at Flamborough and four alighted. On 5 January 1970 these closures took effect, and Flamborough closed entirely, having ceased to handle goods traffic on 10 August 1964.

Some of the economies in line with Fiennes's recommendations of 1967 have been made. Route singling has taken place, from Bridlington to Filey in 1973 and northward to Seamer Junction a decade later, and work was undertaken in the 1980s to introduce unstaffed level crossings. Most of the stations have ceased to be staffed. Flamborough station building remains in residential use, and the adjoining up platform is extant. It is ironic that since its closure the lightly populated surroundings of the station have changed dramatically. Directly north-east is a 26-acre industrial site occupied by a maltings, and immediately south is a mobile home park, with the northern suburbs of Bridlington extending to within a few hundred yards of the station.

SINDERBY (1852)

Date opened	25 May 1852
Location	Beneath and immediately east of A1(M)
Company on opening	Leeds Northern Railway
Date closed to passengers	1 January 1962
Date closed completely	11 November 1963
Company on closing	British Railways (North Eastern Region)
Present state	Demolished
County	Yorkshire North Riding (now North Yorkshire)
OS grid ref	SE334812

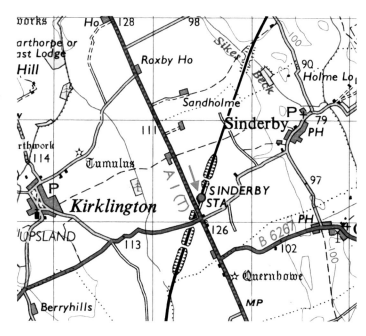

The Leeds & Thirsk Railway (L&TR) obtained an Act on 21 July 1845 to construct its main line, with connections to the Leeds & Bradford Railway and branches to Knaresborough and into Harrogate. The line opened in stages; first was Ripon-Thirsk, to minerals on 5 January 1848 and all traffic on 1 June 1848. On 1 September 1848 Weeton (south of Harrogate) to Wormald Green via Starbeck opened; this was followed by Wormald Green to Ripon 12 days later. The southward continuation eventually opened on 9 July 1849 to a temporary terminus in Leeds at Wellington Street. The present-day station in central Harrogate opened on 1 August 1862. In 1846 the L&TR sought powers to extend its rails north from Melmerby to Stockton-on-Tees, passing under the Great North of England Railway (GNoER, which was to become part of the East Coast Main Line) at Northallerton. In 1848 the L&TR received parliamentary approval to build its route, opposition from the GNoER to the Melmerby-Northallerton section having been overcome. It was to include 2¼ miles of earthworks north from Melmerby that had been constructed for the abortive Northern Counties Union Railway,

authorised in July 1846, which would have stretched to Kirkby Stephen.

The Melmerby-Stockton line opened on 25 May 1852, by which time the now inappropriately named L&TR had become the Leeds Northern Railway; in 1854 this company became part of the NER, but railwaymen continued to refer to the route as the 'Leeds Northern'. The junction station at Melmerby (named Wath until 1852) was already open, and stations on the southern part of the new route were provided at Sinderby, Newby Wiske and

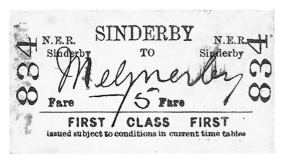

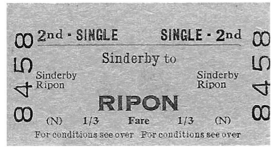

storey stationmaster's house at the north end, under a pitched roof, then a single-storey booking office and waiting room, also with a pitched roof, and a flat-roofed toilet block at the south end. Red brick was used, and stone quoins were the only hint of ornamentation. A timber waiting room with a glazed front was placed at the southern end of the higher, extended platform, close to the main building. In 1901, when the route was doubled by the NER, a second platform was added on the up side, displaced slightly south of the extended down platform, and it also received a timber shelter. The goods yard was behind the up platform, entered from the north, and it included a coal depot but no goods shed. A loading dock and cattle pens were provided on the up side at the south end of the station; the dock was extended northwards to form the new up platform in 1901. A signal box north of the new platform controlled access to the goods yard. In 1913 the yard's principal traffic was barley and livestock.

Bradshaw of February 1863 shows that the Melmerby-Northallerton route operated as a branch, with southbound weekday departures from Sinderby at 8.17am and 7.52pm, both connecting at Melmerby with trains to Leeds; northbound departures were at 9.26am and 8.15pm, with connections from Leeds at Melmerby. No trains ran on

Northallerton Town, to which Northallerton Low (beside the GNoER 'main-line' station) was added in December 1854, and Pickhill in March 1875. Although goods and passenger trains through Sinderby began on 25 May 1852, the full service officially began on 2 June.

The new line through Sinderby was single track, and initially there was one low platform, but when it was lengthened and raised to normal height the original low platform was retained in front of the building. It is thought that the stations on the Melmerby-Stockton line were jointly the work of engineers Thomas Grainger and his successor, John Bourne. The L-plan main building at Sinderby, on the down (northbound) side, was constructed in 1854 and comprised a two-

Sinderby: The station is seen in 1962, shortly after it closed to passengers. This northward view from the A1 road bridge shows the main building with the original low platform in front, extended north-eastwards at standard height.
Stations UK

Sinderby: In June1975 the station, used by an agricultural machinery supplier, is seen from the same 1962 viewpoint. The line through the station was abandoned in 1967 and the rails were removed in 1970. *Alan Young*

Sunday. In October 1898 southbound trains left for Ripon at 7.53am, 10.58am and 2.53pm (the latter on Thursday only, for Ripon's market day), and at 7.58pm to Melmerby. Northbound departures to Northallerton were at 9.20am, 4.05pm (Thursday only) and 8.25pm. Whereas trains stopped at Sinderby every weekday, Pickhill, the next station to the north, was one of a select few in Yorkshire used only on market days, with calls on Wednesday (for Northallerton market) and Thursday (Ripon's market day) in 1898. Wassand (Hull-Hornsea), Wilstrop Siding (Harrogate-York) and West Rounton Gates (Northallerton-Stockton) were stations with similarly restricted services.

Doubling of the Melmerby-Northallerton tracks in 1901 enabled the line to be used for express trains between Leeds, Harrogate,

Sinderby: Looking south-west at the main building in June 1975. *Alan Young*

Northallerton and points north; it was 3 miles shorter than the route via Thirsk, and avoided such trains occupying some miles of the increasingly congested East Coast Main Line between Thirsk and Northallerton. This project also enabled trains on the Sinderby route to use the main-line Northallerton station, via the new Cordio Loop, and the lower station in Northallerton was closed. However, the service pattern for local trains gave preference to the route via Thirsk, which served a larger population; the winter 1937-38 timetable shows three weekday calls in each direction at Sinderby, while four used the route via Thirsk.

Some stations encouraged the growth of housing and industry in their vicinity, but

Sinderby failed to do this, and the small village from which it took its name was a mile away. No large settlements lay within its catchment area, and NER records show that in 1911 the station served only 963 people and issued 6,040 tickets. Despite being lightly used, Sinderby survived into the British Railways era with a threadbare service that, in the summer of 1954, amounted to one southbound and two northbound departures. From September 1955 Sinderby was left with just one departure, the southbound 7.24am. On 14 September 1959 the 'old' route between Melmerby and Thirsk was closed completely, having latterly been operated as a single-track line, the other track being used for wagon storage. Sinderby kept its single morning train (diesel-operated by June 1959), whose primary purpose was to unload mail and parcels, until the station closed to passengers on 1 January 1962. The other stations between Melmerby and Northallerton predeceased Sinderby, Newby Wiske closing to passengers in 1939 and Pickhill in 1959. Goods traffic was handled at Sinderby until 11 November 1963.

The Harrogate-Northallerton railway was earmarked for closure in the Beeching Report, by which time service frequency in each direction was approximately 2-hourly, and

Sinderby: The station stood in the way of the engineering work involved in upgrading the A1 to motorway standard. In March 2009 the trackbed has been filled to platform level and the redundant building awaits its fate. *Neil Cholmondeley*

the only train of distinction using the route was the London King's Cross-Glasgow 'Queen of Scots' Pullman. Closure of the line took place on 6 March 1967, and the section from Melmerby Ordnance Depot through Sinderby to Northallerton closed completely on this day.

Following an accident on the East Coast Main Line on 31 July 1967 the 'Leeds Northern' reopened for diverted northbound trains until 2 August. The line had proved its value as an emergency route, and voices were raised in a vain endeavour to keep it open. However, there were so few serious accidents on the main line that it was considered uneconomic to maintain

Sinderby: By October 2009 the single-storey section of the building had been demolished. *Neil Cholmondeley*

the route for occasional diversions. The A1
road bridge over the railway at Sinderby was
condemned as unsafe by BR, perhaps as a
device to justify the line's abandonment, and in
1968 it was infilled without removing the tracks.
The Melmerby-Ripon line was out of use by
April 1969, and on 9 October of that year the
final goods train ran on the route south from
Ripon. The 'Leeds Northern' rails were lifted in
1970.

For many years Sinderby station was
owned by an agricultural machinery supplier,
and the main building and both platforms
survived long after closure. From December
2002 a diesel locomotive – No 47540 *The
Institution of Civil Engineers* – and a number
of Mark II coaches were stored on a short
length of track behind the station for future
preservation. However, no work was done;
the coaches were removed for scrapping in
2009, and the locomotive was transferred to
the Wensleydale Railway, a project referred to

Sinderby: In September 2010 a short section
of platform on the extreme right, beside the
warning cones, is all that remains of the station. *Neil
Cholmondeley*

in the section on Aysgarth. For more than 50
years the process of rebuilding the A1 road to
motorway standard has been going on, and the
section past Sinderby station has now been
upgraded. The station building, which had been
empty for some time, stood in the way of the
motorway and was demolished in October
2009. Neil Cholmondeley's splendid series of
photographs provides a valuable record of the
station's demise. Although a feasibility study for
reopening the Harrogate-Northallerton line
has been carried out, no progress has been
made with what would be an expensive project.
Ripon would be the only place of importance
to which trains would be restored.

SLEDMERE & FIMBER (1853)

Date opened	1 June 1853
Location	South side of B1251 road at former level crossing
Company on opening	Malton & Driffield Junction Railway
Date closed to passengers	5 June 1950
Date closed completely	2 October 1958
Company on closing	British Railways (North Eastern Region)
Present state	Little evidence remains, but small section of rear of platform survives. Fimber Road crossing-keeper's house is in private occupation at east end of station.
County	Yorkshire East Riding (now East Riding of Yorkshire)
OS grid ref	SE908610

The Yorkshire Wolds form a scimitar curve from the coast at Flamborough Head to the Humber near Brough. These are chalk hills, rolling and rounded, but broken up by deep and surprisingly remote dry valleys. Although the architecture of the widely spaced villages is unmistakably northern, the landscape that surrounds them is reminiscent of the downs in Berkshire and Wiltshire. Anyone who visits the sites of the seven stations on the former Malton & Driffield Junction Railway (M&DJR), all inconveniently placed to serve the villages whose names they carried, might

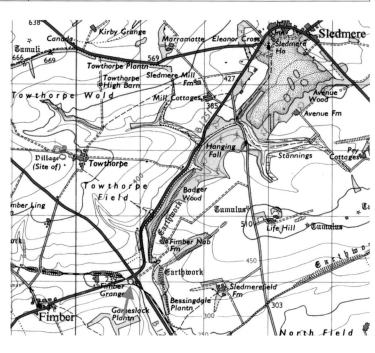

wonder why this area was considered worthy of a line that required substantial engineering works, including the 1,746-yard Burdale Tunnel. However, the railway was conceived as a double-track trunk route to link the Northumberland and Durham coalfield with the port of Hull: Burton (1997) remarks that it was originally proposed to call it the Newcastle upon Tyne & Hull Direct Railway, and describes it as a 'main line that never was'. The line was locally promoted but had the approval of

George Hudson, whose embryonic East Coast Main Line would provide the crucial link to the northern coalfield. The M&DJR received the Royal Assent on 26 June 1846.

Several major deficiencies scuppered its chances of becoming a trunk route. Its intended junction at Malton faced away from the proposed Thirsk & Malton line, which was to give access to the main line and the coalfield; at Driffield its junction would face north, rather than towards Hull; and the route was steeply

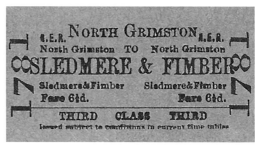

graded (reaching 1 in 67) and abounded in tight curves. Moreover, the difficulties of building through the hard chalk were underestimated. Construction began at an unfavourable time, coinciding with a financial crisis when the heady days of 'Railway Mania' suddenly ended, and with Hudson's disgrace and downfall. Money was saved by proceeding with a single-track railway, and thus a narrower Burdale Tunnel, and by diverting the line at its northern end, which placed it further than intended from Settrington and North Grimston villages. The grand opening ceremony of the 19½-mile line eventually took place on 19 May 1853, with the public service starting on 1 June. The Thirsk-Malton line opened to passengers at the same time. Unfortunately there was an inconvenient railway layout at Malton, where Thirsk to Driffield trains had to set back into Malton before changing direction once more to continue to Driffield.

M&DJR stations were very much an afterthought, and in 1846 the directors stated that 'no buildings of great consequence or elaborate architecture will be required'. This was in contrast to the neighbouring York-Scarborough line, which benefited from Andrews's station buildings, such as at Castle Howard – and the post 'Mania' financial stringencies had yet to arise. The contract for the buildings was awarded to bricklayer William Clark and carpenter Matthew Hewson, both of Driffield. Thus Sledmere & Fimber and the other stations received unpretentious buildings resembling the local farmhouses that the contractors would have been used to building. They were of red brick with pitched slate roofs, and only the projecting corbels at the gable ends added a touch of refinement. The stations were broadly similar, but later alterations, in Burton's words, created 'a hotch-

Sledmere & Fimber: Looking south-east in the 1950s, the station building and the platform can be seen, the latter shortened after closure to passengers. *J. W. Armstrong Photographic Trust*

Sledmere & Fimber: Seen in April 1976, the station building is derelict with the windows boarded up and the platform overgrown. *Alan Young*

potch of buildings, and all very different'. As built they contained a station office, living room and kitchen on the ground floor, as well as a scullery, wash house, pantry, coalhole and privy; upstairs there were two bedrooms. The platforms were economically built, short and barely 18 inches high. Only North Grimston station received entirely new and improved buildings, in 1895, to placate Lord Middleton, who was dissatisfied with his local station's facilities.

Sledmere & Fimber station was a mile from the hamlet of Fimber and 3 miles from Sledmere village. At first its name was Fimber, but from March 1858 precedence was given to Sledmere as it served Sir Tatton Sykes's residence of Sledmere House, and he was an enthusiastic supporter and shareholder in the M&DJR project. In May 1859 it became Sledmere & Fimber. The single platform and building were on the up (south) side of the two tracks at the station. Sykes had a private waiting room, but in 1860 he waived this privilege on condition that it would in future be for 1st Class passengers only; this is probably what later became the ladies' waiting room. Rearrangement of the office and waiting facilities in the station building took place, and

at some stage a lean-to kitchen was added. In the late 19th century the NER provided an enclosed pent-roofed wooden waiting shed just east of the main building, and the platform was heightened and lengthened, but (as at Sinderby) the original low platform was retained in front of the main building. Also on the platform was the only proper signal box at any of the stations – the others having ground frames – and in 1876 a small lock-up warehouse was built.

Despite its remote location this was considered the principal station on the line, and its goods facilities were generous. The RCH *Handbook* of 1904 reports that the full range of standard goods traffic could be handled. In 1912 Sledmere's goods receipts were three times its revenue from passengers, and the principal commodities dispatched were grain (barley, wheat and oats), timber from the Sledmere estate and livestock. A 1935 plan shows that the down-side track was not for through traffic but gave access to the goods facilities, with five sidings east of the level crossing, where there were two goods docks, a weighing machine and coal depot. The line's most substantial warehouse was provided here, a two-storey structure whose size reflected the needs of the Sledmere estate and the importance of the local grain fields. A short siding, which had a 3-ton crane, extended west of the level crossing. Twice a year Sykes's stable used the goods facilities to transport horses to

Sledmere & Fimber: The station building is seen from the road in February 1978, a short time before it was demolished. *Alan Lewis*

Newmarket race meetings. In addition to the goods facilities the station supported local needs by serving as the local sub-post office. Although not dealt with at Sledmere, stone traffic was important on the Malton-Driffield line, supplied by several quarries including those at Wharram and Burdale.

Bradshaw of February 1863 shows three weekday departures in each direction from Sledmere at approximately 5-hour intervals, two of which ran to or from Thirsk, and no Sunday trains. In the winter of 1912-13 three trains ran each way daily, with a further afternoon working on Tuesday, Thursday and Saturday, providing transport to the Tuesday and Thursday markets at Driffield and the Saturday market at Malton. Although population was sparse and passenger traffic was always light, Hoole (1974) reminds us that in the days before motor transport the Malton-Driffield line was the only means by which local people could reach either of the town's markets, and this was especially true in winter when the hilly roads became blocked with deep snowdrifts but the trains kept running, albeit sometimes with difficulty. Nevertheless the stationmaster at Burdale, the most isolated on the line, apparently kept three months' stock of food! As noted earlier, Sledmere was the busiest of the seven wayside stations, but in 1911 only 1,108 people lived within its hinterland and 6,546 tickets were booked; Wetwang was second in importance, with 5,219. Garton, the quietest station, booked only 2,065 passengers in that year.

Faced with the drift of passengers from rail to road transport, the Thirsk-Malton line ceased to carry passengers between Gilling and Malton in 1931. As with the Malton-Driffield line, its stations were inconveniently sited for the villages along the main road that ran parallel to the railway. However, Malton-Driffield survived the LNER's outburst of closures of 1929-31, reflecting the superiority of this admittedly steeply graded route over the local roads. The LNER winter 1937-38 timetable shows which stations were served by 'associated' bus companies, and significantly only two of the intermediate stations, Settrington and North Grimston, enjoyed this privilege. Three trains operated daily at this time, departing from Sledmere to Driffield at 7.36am, 11.03am and 6.16pm, and to Malton at 9.18am, 12.53pm and 7.21pm, a couple of coaches proving more than sufficient for the limited number of passengers. At many stations in North East England staff

Sledmere & Fimber: In February 1978 the station's waiting shed is seen in use as a pavilion at a nearby cricket ground. *Alan Lewis*

Above: **Sledmere & Fimber:** The former grain warehouse is derelict and awaiting demolition in February 1978. *Alan Lewis*

Right: **Sledmere & Fimber:** The course of the former line through the passenger station and goods yard is seen in September 2008. *Nick Catford*

lovingly tended the gardens, and from time to time special excursions visited this line for passengers to admire their handiwork. Sledmere station also welcomed distinguished visitors. In the 1880s Queen Victoria used the station when visiting Sledmere House, and on 6 July 1948 the Royal Train brought King George VI, Queen Elizabeth and Princess Margaret to Sledmere for the same purpose, and all regular trains that day were cancelled. After the Royal party alighted, their train was shunted into a siding and a rail temporarily removed to prevent other trains from accidentally colliding with it.

By 1940 the cost of staffing the stations had been reduced by retaining stationmasters only at North Grimston and Sledmere, the latter also supervising Wetwang and Garton to the east. The line survived into the BR era, and there was a glimpse of the 'trunk route' status to which it had aspired when summer Saturday trains worked via Sledmere, including expresses to and from Filey Holiday Camp. The Winter 1949-50 timetable shows three trains each way on weekdays, the first in each direction running to or from Bridlington. This was to be the final season, for the 'Malton Dodger', the name by which local people affectionately knew their train, passed into history on Saturday 3 June 1950, the last day of service. An account of journeys on the last day by Chris Wilson, then a pupil at Ampleforth, is included in Burton's book, evoking the character of this charming rural line with its wonderful 'blossom-filled

Sledmere & Fimber: A group of Yorkshire Wolds Railway volunteers are seen with the short stretch of track close to the former station on 21 June 2014. They are pictured with GEC Traction 0-4-0 diesel-hydraulic locomotive No 5576, built for Shotton steelworks and restored for work on the Yorkshire Wolds Railway. *Matthew Brown*

chalky valley' through Sledmere. 'G4' 0-4-4T No 67293 hauled the final trains.

Goods trains continued on the whole line and served Sledmere, and on at least two occasions passenger services were restored when local roads were blocked by snow on 12-16 February 1953 and in the winter of 1957-58; it is not known which stations temporarily reopened for these trains. Scenic excursions also occasionally visited the line. In anticipation of its complete closure the M&DJR welcomed enthusiasts' special trains organised by the Branch Line Society and the RCTS on 2 and 23 June 1957 respectively. In the late 1950s the goods service was limited to one

train each way on Tuesday and Thursday only. The last goods ran on Saturday 18 October 1958, and the line was officially closed two days later. The tracks were soon removed, although short stretches remained at Malton and Driffield for some years. The timber waiting shed from Sledmere was removed to the local cricket ground to serve as a pavilion until it was destroyed by fire. The station building and goods warehouse were neglected and their dilapidated remains were pulled down in 1978. The cleared site is now a picnic area with a log cabin serving refreshments in summer. The Yorkshire Wolds Railway restoration project was established in 2008 with a plan to rebuild some of the former Malton-Driffield railway and operate a steam-hauled passenger service. At present 100 yards of track has been laid immediately east of the site of Sledmere & Fimber station, and it is intended soon to extend this to Wetwang.

STEPNEY (1853)

Date opened	1 June 1853
Location	West side of Beverley Road, Hull
Company on opening	York & North Midland Railway
Date closed to passengers	19 October 1964
Date closed completely	6 September 1965
Company on closing to passenger services	British Railways (North Eastern Region)
Company on closing to goods services	British Rail (North Eastern Region)
Present state	Station building and both platforms survive
County	Yorkshire East Riding (now East Riding of Yorkshire)
OS grid ref	TA089302

Between Flamborough Head and the Humber is Holderness, a triangular tract of almost level, fertile land with numerous villages and a few towns: Beverley and Driffield inland, and the resorts of Withernsea, Hornsea and Bridlington on the coast. For this survey, two stations have been selected on the former Withernsea and Hornsea branches. Stepney was on the route through the northern suburbs of Hull, used by trains on both branches as far as Wilmington, where they parted company, and it has been chosen for its attractive architecture, which can still be appreciated.

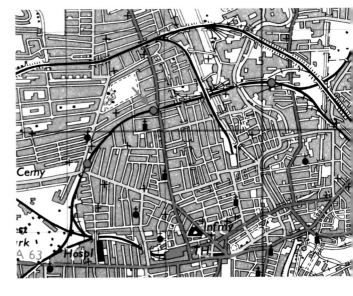

The other is Rye Hill & Burstwick (see next section), typical of the building style on the Withernsea branch. Only a year separated the opening of these two stations, so they appear in sequence.

The York & North Midland Railway (Y&NMR) served Hull's town docks on the western side of the River Hull. However, after Victoria Dock on the east side of Hull opened in 1850, a new railway was needed to serve it. The Victoria Dock branch line was just over 3 miles long, running in roughly a semicircle from Anlaby Road (junction with the Hull-Selby line) north of Hull and terminating at the dock; powers were obtained for its construction in June 1852, and it opened to freight on 16 May 1853. The line had level crossings over several main roads. A suburban passenger service – one of the earliest in the country – began on 1 June 1853, but lasted only into 1854 as it was poorly patronised. At this time Hull's built-up area stopped short of Stepney.

The Hull & Holderness Railway (H&HR) was incorporated on 8 July 1853 and consisted of an 18-mile route from Victoria Dock station to the small coastal town of Withernsea. The

Stepney: This general view is looking south-west, probably in the late 1930s. The fine Italianate building designed by William Botterill is on the up (left) platform, with humbler NER timber structures on the down platform. An LNER nameboard is fixed to the main building. *John Mann collection*

errain enabled the line to be built rapidly, and it opened on 27 June 1854. The company struggled financially and from the start of 1860 the line was worked by the NER; on 17 July 1862 it became wholly NER-owned. The original H&HR Act enabled the company to provide a route into Hull Paragon, the town's major station, and the NER swiftly revived the powers and built a curve that allowed trains from Withernsea to terminate there from 1 June 1864. The Hornsea branch had opened on 28 March 1864, and stopped short of Hull at Wilmington station, situated adjacent to the Victoria Dock branch. From 1 June 1864 trains from this branch were also extended into Paragon station via the Victoria Dock branch. Stepney reopened on this date to be served by Withernsea and Hornsea trains.

Earlier sections of this book have included railways in George Hudson's 'empire', including the Y&NMR, where the station buildings were the work of the architect G. T. Andrews. Stepney station was designed by William Botterill, who

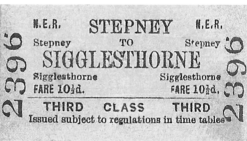

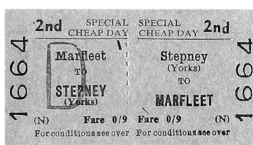

was clerk of works under Andrews when Hull's Royal Station Hotel was under construction in 1849. Botterill set up an architectural practice in 1851 and favoured building in the Italianate style. Stepney station was immediately west

of the Beverley Road level crossing and had two facing platforms. The main building, on the south platform, was a lively yet dignified design a two-storey Italianate red-brick structure with grey-brick pilaster stripes, and projecting

Above: **Stepney:** Looking north-east on 6 September 1956, the Y&NMR building is accompanied by gas lamps and a 'coiled serpent' bench, a favoured design found on many NER stations. *John Mann collection*

Below: **Stepney:** On 17 October 1964, the final day of Hull to Hornsea and Withernsea passenger trains 'WD' locomotive heads a westbound freight train in the unstaffed station. *G. C. Lewthwaite*

Stepney:
The southern
and eastern
elevations of the
building in April
1976. *Alan Young*

gables at each end. The stone-trimmed windows were round-headed and there was an elegant centrally placed stone arched porch on the platform elevation; this, at least in later years, enclosed a window rather than a door. The roof had an overhang and was topped by coupled chimneystacks. Single-storey gabled wings extended parallel to the platform on both flanks of the building. On the north platform there was a long timber building under a ridged roof providing waiting accommodation. At the east end of the platforms a footbridge enabled pedestrians to cross the line when the gates were closed and to transfer between platforms. A signal box was situated immediately east of the crossing, north of the tracks. The goods facilities shown on the OS Town Plan of 1892 comprised four sidings south of the passenger station, entered from the west. One served a timber yard and two served the coal depot. A 2-ton 10cwt crane was installed. However, by 1910 the goods sidings had been removed, and the 1928 OS plan shows a billiard hall and a picture theatre occupying their site. Further east was a goods depot, part of Sculcoates station (closed to passengers in 1912) but named Stepney goods yard on the 1928 plan.

In many respects the branches to Withernsea and Hornsea were twins, with no particularly large settlements to serve after Hull until they reached their termini, and their train services were remarkably similar. In July 1896,

for example, seven weekday trains departed from Stepney for each branch (together with some operating on one day only or 'when necessary'), and there were three Sunday departures for each, three of which returned from Hornsea and four from Withernsea. By this date housing had engulfed the fields close to the station, but Hull's built-up area came to an end less than a quarter of a mile to the north. In 1911 Stepney issued 45,569 tickets.

When the NER became part of the new LNER in 1923 Stepney's weekday service was between eight and 11 trains in each direction on each branch, with three down Sunday trains to each of Withernsea and Hornsea, and four trains from each branch towards Hull. In July 1938 the frequency had increased to about a dozen trains serving each branch on weekdays in each direction. Under BR(NE) administration from 1948 little was done to modernise Stepney station, with gas lighting retained. Wooden running-in nameboards were painted tangerine, but no additional name signage was provided.

Trains on the Hornsea and Withernsea branches were steam-hauled until 7 January 1957 when diesel multiple units were introduced, providing all services by the end of that summer. On 4 January 1960 the North Eastern Region took the unprecedented step of making both branches 'Paytrain' lines, to use a term that BR adopted some years later. At every intermediate station between Hull and the Withernsea and Hornsea termini (except Hornsea Bridge) booking offices were closed and the stations became 'unstaffed halts' – although the NE Region did not add 'Halt' to their names, as by this time the policy was to limit the suffix to 'untimetabled' stations, such as Melton Halt, described later. Tickets were issued by the conductor/guard on the train to passengers joining at unstaffed stations. This was a cost-saving exercise but, although fewer station staff had to be paid, numerous attended level crossings remained. Bairstow (2002) notes that the Centralised Traffic Control Scheme (CTC), which was to be tested on the York-Beverley route, was intended ultimately to reach the Withernsea branch, starting at Hedon, and the Hornsea branch starting at Wilmington, with a control centre at Hull; both branches would be singled, level crossings automated and many signal boxes closed. However, the Beeching Report listed both branches for closure, and the official

Below: **Stepney:** In July 2014 the station building looks splendid and both platforms are intact. *Mark Dyson*

Above: **Stepney:** The southern elevation in July 2014. *Mark Dyson*

proposal was published with almost indecent haste on 12 July 1963. The expense of traditional operation was used to justify their closure – the intention to adopt CTC having been abandoned – regardless of the savings made by de-staffing stations and the introduction of modern trains that, invariably, attracted more passengers. On 4 January 1964 the TUCC heard more than 80 objections, and a petition signed by 15,000 holidaymakers was submitted. A case was made that Withernsea depended heavily on the railway to bring in day visitors; about 35,000 passengers per month travelled in the summer peak season, with an annual total of some 132,000. However, only about 200 local people used the line to commute to Hull.

On 31 July 1964 Ernest Marples, Secretary of State for Transport, approved closure to Hornsea and Withernsea, to take place on 19 October. A General Election date had been announced for Thursday 15 October, and while the Conservative Government had appointed Beeching to his role as BR Chairman and provided his remit to pursue a programme of passenger closures – and Marples had personal business motives for favouring road transport over rail – the Labour opposition had intimated that it would look more favourably on retaining the railway infrastructure with a moratorium on 'major' closures. Labour was victorious, albeit by a very narrow margin, and Thompson (1992) and Bairstow (1995) describe a frantic last-minute attempt to prevent the closure of the Withernsea and Hornsea lines. A telegram was sent to the new Prime Minister, Harold Wilson, by the Clerk to Hornsea UDC: 'Hornsea and Withernsea branch lines close tomorrow night. Request you intervene to halt closure.' Commander Harry Pursey, Hull East Labour MP, travelled to London to lobby for the retention of the branches. All of this was to no avail. Passenger services were withdrawn on Monday 19 October 1964, the final trains having run two days earlier. To the last the branches retained a respectable service, with between eight and ten departures from Stepney in each direction for each branch, and a higher frequency, including Sunday trains, in the final summer of operation. It was soon apparent that the Labour Government intended to continue the closure programme, and hopes of reopening the branches were dashed.

In May 1965 goods services ended on the Hornsea branch, apart from trains conveying chalk to a cement mill near Wilmington station. Stepney (formerly Sculcoates) goods station closed on 6 September 1965 according to Clinker's Register, but the Grade II building survives and is used as a haulage depot by European Road Freight Ltd. Goods services continued on the Withernsea branch as far as Hedon until 3 June 1968, and were then cut back to Marfleet until 1 May 1972, when this section of line closed. On 28 October 1968 the former Victoria Dock branch through Stepney was closed entirely as Hull Corporation and BR

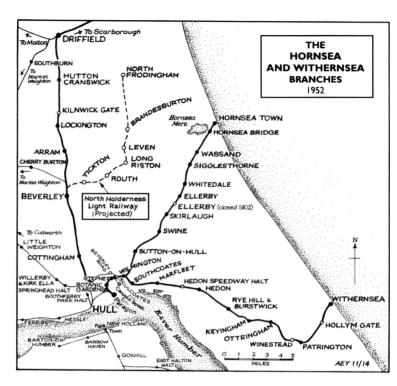

Stepney: This map shows Stepney's relation to the Hornsea and Withernsea branches. *Alan Young*

were keen to abolish the many level crossings that caused traffic congestion and required staffing. Goods traffic to and from the east of Hull was diverted onto the former H&BR route, which ran at a higher elevation, with bridges rather than level crossings. A spur was constructed to the Hornsea branch to make this possible but in the event it was used for only three years.

In general, suburban stations have not survived long after closure. Unless their buildings are suitable for adaptation to residential or business premises they fall prey to vandals, and property developers recognise the potential of their sites. Stepney is an exception, and its building survives in an excellent state of preservation complete with platforms. A pedestrian and cycle route occupies the trackbed.

RYE HILL & BURSTWICK (1854)

Date opened	27 June 1854
Location	South-east side of Station Road at former level crossing
Company on opening	Hull & Holderness Railway
Date closed to passengers	19 October 1964
Date closed completely	3 May 1965
Company on closing to passenger services	British Railways (North Eastern Region)
Company on closing to goods services	British Rail (North Eastern Region)
Present state	Station building/stationmaster's house is a private residence and platform survives; other platform is heavily overgrown alongside cycleway
County	Yorkshire East Riding (now East Riding of Yorkshire)
OS grid ref	TA225270

The Hull & Holderness Railway (H&HR) was promoted by Hull merchant Anthony Bannister to link the industrial port of Hull with the agricultural land of south Holderness; parts of this region had been accessible via the River Humber at Hedon and Patrington havens, but these had begun to silt up. A secondary objective was to develop a seaside resort in much the same way as the York & North Midland Railway (Y&NMR) had begun to develop Scarborough and Whitby. The coast between Tunstall and Easington was surveyed and Withernsea was chosen to be the terminus of the line, and the new resort.

Receiving the Royal Assent on 8 July 1853, the line was easy to construct as the region is almost flat, and ballast could be extracted close to the line at Kelsey Hill, near Burstwick. The line opened on 30 June 1854 with its Hull terminus at Victoria Dock station.

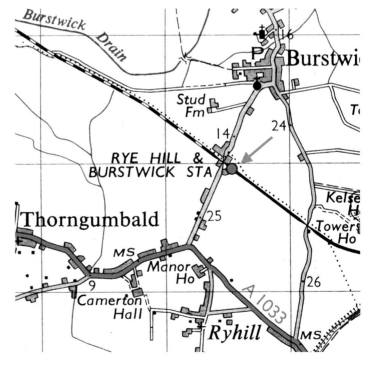

At first the railway was completely independent with its own rolling stock; however, on 1 January 1860 it was leased to the NER, which bought it outright on 7 July 1862. Trains were

Right: **Rye Hill & Burstwick:**
By the time of this photograph, looking south-east in 1962, the station was unstaffed. The building, of a distinctive design by Thomas Cabry, was found at several other stations on the former Hull & Holderness Railway. *Stations UK*

Above: **Rye Hill & Burstwick:** The down platform, station building and goods shed are seen in April 1976. *Alan Young*

diverted to Paragon station on 1 June 1864. The route was single track but most of it was doubled early in the 20th century, although Hedon to Rye Hill & Burstwick and Ottringham to Winestead remained single.

Although Withernsea station was a 'low, mean building' (Fawcett 2001), the wayside stations were a different matter, 'combining economy with an ingenious and effective layout'. They were designed by Thomas Cabry, Engineer to the Y&NMR, and he was permitted by his employer to work privately as Engineer to the H&HR. Rye Hill station's building on the north-east (down) platform was typical of these wayside examples. A red-brick two-storey villa aligned parallel to the platform was the centrepiece, beneath a slate ridged roof with generous overhangs. The upper storey had

rectangular window openings, with only two surprisingly small ones overlooking the platform. A brick-built verandah with a hipped slate roof, thrust forward like an apron, made the building distinctive, and waiting rooms were built as cross-arms at each end. The ground-floor windows on the side elevation were round-headed. On the facing up platform was a pent-roofed timber waiting shelter. Two sidings behind the down platform were entered from the south-east, and NER records for 1913 indicate that wheat and livestock were the principal goods traffic. The goods shed was immediately south-east of the main building with a cattle pen close by. The signal box was on the down platform adjacent to the level crossing.

The station stood between the two villages of Rye Hill and Burstwick, each about half a mile away. It was called Burstwick until 1 July 1881 when it became Rye Hill, then from 23

Right: **Rye Hill & Burstwick:** Although the verandah has now been enclosed, the building retains much of its character, and the platform is still in place in July 2014. *Mark Dyson*

September 1929 it was Rye Hill & Burstwick. Official sources suggest that Rye Hill, rather than Ryehill, was the preferred form of the name, although LNER running-in nameboards used the latter version. The 1955 OS 1-inch map shows the village to be spelled Ryhill. There was little population close to the station, and in 1911 it served a catchment of only 942; that year 11,205 tickets were booked. After the Second World War detached houses were built north of the station on the road to Burstwick.

In February 1863 the station had four weekday departures to Withernsea and to Hull Victoria, together with one on Tuesday only to Withernsea; two trains called in each direction on Sunday. In July 1896 the frequency had increased to seven towards Withernsea on most weekdays, but eight on Saturday, and nine on Tuesday for passengers returning from Hull on market day; eight trains departed on weekdays for Hull Paragon and three trains called each way on Sunday. Under LNER ownership a reasonably frequent service was provided in the winter of 1937-38, with between 10 and 13 departures each way on weekdays and three on Sunday. During the Second World War the frequency decreased to eight in each direction on weekdays and two on Sunday.

Under BR North Eastern Region Rye Hill & Burstwick generally enjoyed between nine and 15 trains on weekdays, the higher figure being on Saturdays, with three or four departures on summer Sundays. The accompanying 1962 photograph shows a station little changed from Victorian times, still oil-lit, but with an LNER nameboard carrying the station's revised name.

Above: **Rye Hill & Burstwick:** Looking north-west in July 2014, both platforms are extant. The station building can be seen in the background beyond the two modern structures. *Mark Dyson*

As noted in the previous entry, all Hull-Withernsea intermediate stations were de-staffed from 4 January 1960, and the branch closed to passengers on 19 October 1964, a casualty of the Beeching 'axe'. The goods yard closed on 3 May 1965. The station building survived closure and, although there are external alterations including the enclosing of the verandah, it retains its character and is used by a children's nursery. A new house stands beside the down platform on the site of the old goods shed; an iron fence has been installed close to the platform edge. The up platform is heavily overgrown but it still has some signal cable pulleys attached to its face.

Date opened	3 March 1857
Location	About half a mile north of Potto village on Station Lane, just north of junction with Goulton Lane. Buildings and eastbound platform east of former level crossing on Station Lane; westbound platform on opposite side of road
Company on opening	North Yorkshire & Cleveland Railway
Date closed to passengers	14 June 1954
Date closed completely	1 December 1958
Company on closing	British Railways (North Eastern Region)
Present state	Station house with former office range is private residence fronted by part of eastbound platform; westbound platform overgrown and degraded
County	Yorkshire North Riding (now North Yorkshire)
OS grid ref	NZ472046

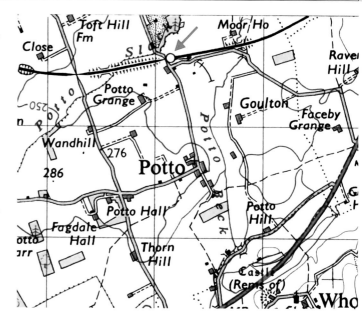

The Leeds & Thirsk Railway (L&TR, later the Leeds Northern Railway) opened its route between these two centres in 1848-49, then in June 1852 extended the line from a junction at Melmerby northwards to Northallerton and Eaglescliffe, just south of Stockton – Sinderby station, described earlier, was on this route. The North Yorkshire & Cleveland Railway (NY&CR), on which Potto was located, branched from the Northallerton-Stockton route at Picton, and was a joint venture between the Leeds Northern and West Hartlepool railways to provide an outlet for the Cleveland ironstone mines on the northern flank of the North York Moors. Authorised in 1854, the NY&CR line from Picton, through Potto, was opened to the public as far as Stokesley on 3 March 1857, a day after the formal opening. At the same time a 2-mile mineral branch south from Potto to Swainby was brought into use to serve Ailesbury ironstone mine. Beyond

Stokesley the route was extended eastwards, opening to goods traffic as far as Ingleby on 1 February 1858 and Kildale on 6 April, and to all traffic to Castleton on 1 April 1861. The line subsequently progressed down the Esk Valley to Grosmont, where it joined the former Whitby & Pickering Railway – described in the Beckhole entry – and this section opened on 2

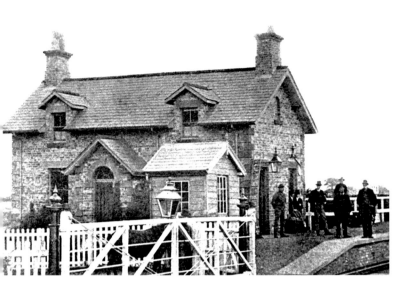

Left: **Potto:** The station building is seen here in its original form before it was raised to two full storeys and the office and waiting room extension was constructed. *Potto Station website*

Below: **Potto:** This tinted postcard view, looking north-east at the Whitby-bound platform circa 1906, shows the additions to the building made by the NER. *Potto Station website*

October 1865.

Potto and its neighbouring stations were designed by John Bourne, Engineer to the L&T and NY&C railways. As originally constructed the building, of dull red brick with stone quoins under a pitched roof, had gabled attic windows on the upper floor and there was an arched porch. The NER later raised the roof to provide a full-size upper storey. The axis of the house was at right-angles to the railway, but the NER added a two-storey extension eastward along the platform and, beyond it, a single-storey office range, both with pitched roofs, and a brick-built store under a hipped roof. These buildings were on the eastbound platform, east of the level crossing. The signal box, an NER addition, was at the crossing adjoining the platform ramp. The platforms were 'staggered', the westbound one being west of the crossing, with a pitched-roof waiting room. The goods dock with a 5-ton yard crane and two sidings were opposite the eastbound platform and, immediately south, a further siding served the coal depot. The

sidings were approached from the mineral branch to Swainby, which left the through line immediately east of Potto station. In 1913 the principal goods traffic handled was hay/clover and livestock. In 1892 the mineral branch from Potto to Swainby closed following the end of mining at Ailesbury.

In February 1863 the NER provided three trains each way on weekdays between Stockton and Castleton, calling at Potto and all other intermediate stations, and one extra westbound on Wednesday morning – market day in Stockton. The winter 1912-13 timetable shows six eastbound departures from Potto

on weekdays, three of which were to Whitby, one to Battersby and two to Middlesbrough; the latter service required a reversal at Battersby to reach Middlesbrough via a link opened to passengers on 1 April 1868. Westbound there were five departures, all to Stockton. As noted earlier, the route through Potto was conceived principally as a mineral line, serving no towns, so passenger traffic was limited; the station at Stokesley, the principal settlement in the area, with fewer than 2,000 residents, was inconveniently situated a mile from the centre of the village. Moreover, while Stockton might have been the regional centre when the railway was opened, in the late 19th century Middlesbrough expanded massively and assumed this role. In 1911 Potto station served a dispersed population of 1,645 and issued 12,133 tickets. In the LNER winter 1937-38 timetable there were four eastbound trains from Potto to Whitby on weekdays, and one that terminated at Battersby, offering connections to Whitby and Middlesbrough; a further Saturday evening train went to Battersby, with a connection to Middlesbrough. Westbound there were five trains to Stockton, one calling at Potto by request.

Potto: On 12 June 1954, the last day of passenger services, Class 'B1' 4-6-0 No 61034 *Chiru* heads the final train to Stockton. *Potto Station website*

The Picton-Battersby line was double track, but from the early 1940s only the eastbound line was used from Picton to Ingleby (three-quarters of a mile west of Battersby); wagons were stored on the westbound line. The road network offered direct access to Middlesbrough and Stockton from the villages served by the NY&CR route, and the railway service declined in frequency as local people preferred to use buses and cars. In the winter of 1953-54 only two trains ran in each direction between Stockton and Whitby. The next BR(NE) timetable, commencing 14 June 1954, showed an improved service, with an additional evening train to Battersby; but this was, in fact, the day when the Picton-Battersby trains were withdrawn, and Potto station closed, together with its neighbours Trenholme Bar, Sexhow, Stokesley and Ingleby. From this date the Esk Valley trains came from Middlesbrough via Nunthorpe and reversed at Battersby, as they still do, to enable them to travel on to Whitby. The Picton-Battersby

Above: **Potto:** Looking west, BR Standard Class 3 No 77012 is on the track into the goods yard, while a rake of wagons occupies the line beyond it. The locomotive was built in June 1954, the month that the station closed to passengers. *J. F. Sedgwick*

Below: **Potto:** What appears to be a Standard Class 3 2-6-0 waits outside the station in September 1958, three months before it closed entirely and the route between Picton and Stokesley was abandoned. *Alan Young collection*

line continued to be used for goods traffic until 1 December 1958, when the section from Picton to Stokesley was abandoned. The tracks were removed from Trenholme Bar through Potto as far as Stokesley in April 1961. The line from Stokesley to Battersby closed entirely

on 2 August 1965. Wagons were stored on the Picton-Trenholme Bar spur until 1971, then the track was removed soon afterwards.

Although the westbound platform of Potto station is degraded and overgrown, east of Station Lane the former station house and

offices survive and retain their character, and a section of platform in front of them also survives. The goods yard is owned by the haulage and logistics firm Preston's of Potto, which, like the owners of the station house, takes a pride in the historic importance of the site. Preston's have preserved the railway yard crane and the weigh office. Although websites are ephemeral, www.pottostation.co.uk is recommended.

Potto: By April 1961, when this photograph was taken, the westbound platform's track had been removed, and within a few weeks the remaining track would be dismantled. The passenger shelter can be seen towards the far end of the platform. *Alan Brown*

Potto: The platform elevation of the building is seen here in February 1990; the old goods dock is in the foreground. *Martin Potter*

Potto: The station building and a section of the Whitby-bound platform are seen in November 2014. *Neil Cholmondeley*

BOWES (1861)

Date opened	8 August 1861
Location	In farmyard east of junction of A66 and A67
Company on opening	South Durham & Lancashire Union Railway
Date closed to passengers	22 January 1962
Date closed completely	22 January 1962
Company on closing	British Railways (North Eastern Region)
Present state	Only fragments remain
County	Yorkshire North Riding (now County Durham)
OS grid ref	NY996138

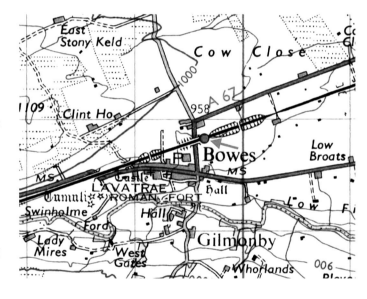

For some miles over the high northern Pennines, the procession of heavy goods vehicles on the A66 road is within sight of a railway that formerly connected Barnard Castle in County Durham with Appleby in Westmorland. The line's summit at Stainmore (1,370 feet) was the highest point reached by a passenger line in England, and just as the A66 in these bleak moorlands is an artery for freight today, so the railway was conceived as a means of hauling industrial raw materials between northern England's west and east coasts. Until the county boundaries were adjusted for administrative convenience in 1974, Bowes was in the North Riding of Yorkshire and Stainmore Summit was in Westmorland (now part of Cumbria).

To the east of the Pennines, the Darlington & Barnard Castle Railway (D&BCR) was opened on 9 July 1856. As described in *Lost Stations of Northumberland & Durham*, in 1856 the South Durham & Lancashire Union Railway (SD&LUR) proposed a line from Bishop Auckland, through Barnard Castle over the Stainmore Pass to join the Lancaster & Carlisle Railway at Tebay (Westmorland). This route would enable iron ore from Whitehaven in

Cumberland and from the Furness district of Lancashire to reach the ironworks of Middlesbrough, while coking coal could be carried in the opposite direction to power the iron industry in the Barrow area. By the time Royal Assent was granted on 13 July 1857 the intention was to provide passenger services too. The engineer for the line was Thomas Bouch, a Cumbrian man whose reputation was later besmirched by the collapse of his Tay Bridge in 1879. Despite the difficult terrain, which required substantial earthworks in places and lofty viaducts over the rivers Tees and Belah and Deepdale Beck, construction of the 35-

mile route from Barnard Castle to Tebay was completed in less than four years. It opened to mineral traffic as far west as Barras on 26 March 1861, then for goods to Tebay on 4 July 1861

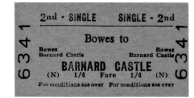

and to passengers throughout on 8 August. A new through station replaced the terminus at Barnard Castle. In 1862 a connecting line was opened from Kirkby Stephen to Penrith by the Eden Valley Railway, and the following year Barnard Castle was connected to Bishop Auckland by the SD&LUR. From the outset the Stockton & Darlington Railway (S&DR) operated the trains, and took control on 30 June 1862; on 13 July 1863 the S&DR became part of the NER. The Barnard Castle to Tebay and Penrith lines were built as single track, but sufficient land was purchased to lay a second track if traffic warranted it. Increasing volumes of freight traffic prompted the NER to double the track in stages from 1867 to 1874, though parts of the Eden Valley line remained single-track. Barrow was the principal industrial area west of the Pennines to benefit from the Stainmore route, but the Cockermouth, Keswick & Penrith line developed a strong association with the 'Stainmore' as it gave access to iron mines and works that were growing in and around Workington.

The village of Bowes is almost 1,000 feet above sea level in the wide valley of the River Greta, a tributary of the Tees. To reach Bowes at a manageable gradient, but still as steep as 1 in 67, the line from Barnard Castle performed a huge reverse curve, gaining almost 400 feet in 6 miles. Beyond Bowes the 10 miles to Barras – probably the longest stretch of railway in England never to have had public stations – was through bleak moorland. The steepest stretch of the route, from Barras to Kirkby Stephen, reached a gradient of 1 in 59.

The SD&LUR stations were designed by Hector Heatley Orrock, an Edinburgh architect who attracted the patronage of Bouch. Fawcett (2003) suggests that their design was strongly influenced by those on the D&BCR, another line engineered by Bouch. Bowes, and most of the other wayside stations, originally consisted of a single-storey, stone-built Tudor Gothic cottage. This was L-shaped, and presented windows to the platform, a square bay window

Bowes: This is the north platform circa 1900, and the elaborate design of the building can be clearly seen. The nameboard – not a standard NER style – competes for attention with the numerous advertising signs, which adorned most stations until the 1930s; these enamel signs are now highly collectable. *Alan Young collection*

Left: **Bowes:** Looking west on 6 May 1962, the abandoned tracks and station can be seen, having closed to all traffic earlier in the year. *Brian Johnson*

Below: **Bowes:** Another view of the main building on the up platform in May 1962. The fascinating design resulted from the NER's additions to H. H. Orrock's original building. *Brian Johnson*

or the office beneath a gable, and a pair of ancets. This gable formed one end of an originally open waiting shed, beyond which was gabled waiting room. The waiting room and he shed had hipped roofs, which produced an unusual but lively profile. The NER expanded he stationmaster's cottage, raising it to two toreys, with two large gables and a tiny one n between, with some cottage orné 'half-imbering' for good measure. The waiting shed vas also given a type of screen found elsewhere on the NER: it was glazed, with panels of wood, rranged in herringbone fashion. The overall esult was a complex and attractive building. he main buildings were on the north (up) latform. The opposite platform had a narrow, tone-built shelter with a hipped roof. It was

originally open, but the NER provided a screen like that on the up platform.

There were four sidings with two loops behind the down platform, which was shortened at its western end where the loops joined the running lines. A loading bank and two further sidings serving the coal depot were south of the loops. Two goods sheds were provided; one of them, of vernacular character resembling local field barns, was provided in preference to the more ambitious design originally intended. The principal goods traffic handled just before the First World War was roadstone and livestock. The signal box was at the east end of the up platform and controlled access to the goods yard. It was of a gabled NER Central Division design with

Left: **Bowes:** The disused station is seen again in May 1962, looking east. The goods depot is on the right. *Brian Johnson*

Below: **Bowes:** After closure the station gradually disintegrated. In August 1976 the roof is losing its slates, but is still substantially intact. The nameboard – now barely legible – is still displayed, and the signal box can be seen at the far end of the platform. *Alan Young*

scalloped bargeboards and a 'scissors truss' providing ornamentation.

The Stainmore line was not expected to carry much passenger traffic, and consequently the service provided was modest. In February 1863 Bradshaw showed two departures from Bowes to Tebay and two to Darlington on weekdays only. In the July 1896 timetable there were five trains in each direction. According to NER statistics for 1911, only 769 people were served by Bowes station and 6,169 tickets were issued – an

very low figure for that time. Although little passenger traffic was generated by the wayside stations, the Stainmore route carried through passenger trains in summer; only three weeks after opening in 1861 an excursion ran over Stainmore from Darlington to Windermere. At the beginning of the 20th century the route remained an important freight carrier. Typically some 20 or more heavily loaded mineral trains worked westwards, while a similar number of freights – goods or empties – travelled east.

In June 1920 three weekday services ran to Tebay and one to Penrith, with four to Darlington; in addition there was one Sunday train to Darlington. During the LNER era a similar weekday service continued, and the

BR(NE) summer 1950 timetable showed little change, with four departures from Bowes in each direction on weekdays, but no Sunday service. However, by this time there was little passenger traffic between Kirkby Stephen and Tebay, and passengers from Bowes had to change at Kirkby Stephen to catch the two trains that served that section of the route.

In 1948 the route from Darlington to Tebay and Penrith, apart from the two western termini, was allocated to BR's North Eastern Region, but in 1950 the London Midland Region assumed control from just east of Kirkby Stephen, and under this administration the Kirkby Stephen-Tebay passenger service was withdrawn. Economies were effected by de-

Right: **Bowes:** Looking west from the down platform in August 1976, the stone-built waiting shelter is in the foreground. *Alan Young*

Below: **Bowes:** The remains of the station building are seen in July 2004. *Alan Young*

staffing Barras station in 1952 and Lartington in 1953. While some rural lines in northern England closed in the 1950s, Stainmore soldiered on. The repainting of Belah Viaduct in 1956 and the transition from steam haulage of passenger trains to diesel multiple units in February 1958 suggested that the line's future was secure. However, in September 1958 two useful trains were cut: the 7.34am Kirkby Stephen-Darlington ceased to run and the 10.34pm (11.00pm on Saturdays) from Darlington no longer travelled as far as Bowes and Kirkby Stephen. On 30 June 1959 the LM and NE regions made a joint submission to the British Transport Commission (BTC) to close the line between Barnard Castle and Penrith to passengers. On 2 October the BTC approved the proposal, and two months later BR announced its intention to close the line. It was noted that DMUs had reduced operating costs, and that their introduction had been followed by an annual increase in receipts of £1,400, but that this improvement had not lasted into 1959. BR believed that diversion of existing Stainmore freight services to alternative routes would save money, particularly as double-heading of trains on the steep gradients was necessary and the volume of freight traffic was declining. In the light of objections, the NW and NE areas' TUCCs recommended postponement of complete closure for 18 months, and testing the practicability of diverting freight to other routes; they also recommended that BR should increase its effort to attract tourists, as they could see the potential for this traffic from rapidly expanding Teesside to the Lake District. Gibbins (2000) expresses surprise that the TUCCs could see increased summer loadings

Bowes: Little is left of the station in September 2007. *Nick Catford*

as the solution to round-the-year losses and that their faith was also placed in 'probable industrial developments'.

In December 1960 a TUCC memo noted that all of the industries involved were satisfied with the diversion of freight from Stainmore, and that there was insufficient potential to justify retention of passenger services on financial grounds. In January 1961 the NW and NE area TUCCs met once more, and while the NW voted for closure the NE voted for retention. The Central TUCC required a decision, and in June 1961 the NE area agreed to closure. Meanwhile in the summer of 1961 passenger services over Stainmore continued with three DMUs each weekday and Saturday-only trains in each direction between North East England and Blackpool via the Tebay line, which had closed to regular passenger traffic. On 7 December 1961 Ernest Marples, Secretary of State for Transport, approved the closure and, as Walton (1992) states, 'with miraculous speed both LM and NE regions announced less than a fortnight later that the last train would run on Saturday 20 January 1962.'

The final scheduled passenger train was the 8.30pm Penrith-Darlington DMU, but an RCTS enthusiasts' steam-hauled special ran from Darlington to Tebay, returning to Kirkby Stephen East before heading to Carlisle. It then followed the final DMU from Penrith and arrived at Darlington at around midnight. On 22 January 1962 the line from Barnard Castle through Bowes to Merrygill Quarry (between Barras and Kirkby Stephen) closed to all traffic, as did the Kirkby Stephen East-Tebay line. The surviving Merrygill Quarry route was cut back to Warcop, between Kirkby Stephen East and Appleby East, on 3 November 1975.

Track removal began almost immediately. While most disused stations have either been completely demolished or renovated and adopted for other uses, Bowes station has gradually disintegrated following closure, with only fragments remaining today. However, further west on the Stainmore route there are two restoration projects offering train journeys for tourists and enthusiasts. The Stainmore Railway Company has restored the station at Kirkby Stephen East, and the Eden Valley Railway Trust, based at Warcop, operates on just over 2 miles of track that it is extending to Appleby East.

KIPLING COTES (1865)

Date opened	1 May 1865
Location	End of short approach road running south from unnamed minor road
Company on opening	North Eastern Railway
Date closed to passengers	29 November 1965
Date closed completely	29 November 1965
Company on closing	British Rail (North Eastern Region)
Present state	Station buildings (extended), goods shed, cattle dock and signal box survive, as do both platforms; south platform is overgrown and retains standards for oil lamp cradles
County	Yorkshire East Riding (now East Riding of Yorkshire)
OS grid ref	SE930439

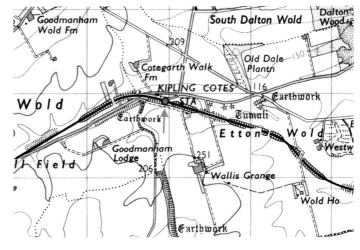

Kipling Cotes station, between Market Weighton and Beverley, was notable for its isolation – in 1911 it served a population of only 127 spread over scattered farms, and issued only 3,011 tickets – and for its longevity – it lasted a century, closing in 1965, after many larger Yorkshire communities had lost their rail service. Close to the station is the starting point of what is possibly the oldest annual horse race in the English sporting calendar, the Kiplingcotes Derby, a 4-mile race over steep, muddy terrain, first held in 1519 and still taking place each spring.

Market Weighton, 3 miles to the west, welcomed its first railway on 4 October 1847 when the York & North Midland reached it from York; on 1 August 1848 the same company's Selby-Market Weighton line followed. It had been the Y&NMR's intention to extend the York line to Beverley (to join the existing route to Hull) and the Selby line to Driffield. However, the Market Weighton-Beverley route crossed the estate of Lord Hotham of Dalton Holme, and his intransigence, coupled with serious financial difficulties faced by

the Y&NMR, frustrated the scheme. Under pressure from local people to build the line, the NER, successor to the Y&NMR, having considered reaching Hull via Brough instead, reverted to the Beverley plan, and an Act of 30 June 1862 approved the project. A condition of building through his land required the NER to provide Lord Hotham with a station at Kipling Cotes.

The Market Weighton-Beverley line was built as single track, and Kipling Cotes station building was on the down (north) side. It resembled those designed by G. T. Andrews for the route opened almost two decades earlier between York and Market Weighton – and

Kipling Cotes: Seen looking south-east on 27 September 1958, the station was built at the behest of Lord Hotham of Dalton Holme, across whose land the railway was built; it stood within sparsely populated countryside in the Wolds, but remained open until 1965. *G. C. Lewthwaite*

Kipling Cotes opened some ten years after his death. The rectangular brick-built two-storey house at Kipling Cotes had its gable end-on to the platform, and a ground floor canted bay window gave the stationmaster a clear view of the platform. Single-storey extensions were provided at each end, one for the booking office and the other for a waiting room. Goods sidings were on the down side, entered from the west and controlled by a ground frame. A brick-built goods shed stood immediately west of the platform, and a cattle dock and a 2-ton crane were installed. In 1913 barley and livestock were the principal goods dealt with. When the line was doubled in 1899, a facing platform with a timber pent-roof waiting shelter was added; passengers used a barrow crossing at the east end to transfer between platforms. At this time a signal box at the west end of the new platform replaced the ground frame.

In July 1896 Kipling Cotes had six weekday departures in each direction; one westbound call was by request only for 1st Class passengers to alight from Beverley or beyond or to join for York or beyond; presumably they would be travelling to or from Lord Hotham's residence. The NER summer 1920 and LNER winter 1937-38 services were only a little less frequent.

This idyllically located station was kept immaculate and provided a setting for such purposes as promoting new rolling stock. It entered the BR era looking essentially as it had done in Victorian times, still oil-lit, and only the wooden nameboards in BR(NE) tangerine were a concession to the mid-20th century. Kipling Cotes survived a proposal in 1958 to close it, although Cherry Burton, its only neighbour on the Market Weighton-Beverley line, closed in 1959. However, on 12 June 1961 Kipling Cotes was downgraded to an unstaffed 'halt', though that suffix was not added.

In the early 1950s the future looked bright for the York-Market Weighton-Beverley line. The first level crossing in Britain with lifting barriers was installed at Warthill in 1953, some colour light signalling appeared, and steel sleepers were laid between Market Weighton and Kipling Cotes. From 29 July 1957 diesel multiple units took over most of the train workings. In 1961 BR decided to operate the line by Centralised Traffic Control from York, reduce most of the route to single track, convert many level crossings to automatic half-barriers, and overhaul the signalling. However, little progress had been made when the Beeching Report earmarked the line – and the Selby-Market Weighton-Driffield route – for closure, and presented it as a case study of a loss-making service. It was asserted that most passengers travelled between York and Hull (but could travel via Selby instead) and that intermediate stations were little used; Kipling Cotes was probably the quietest. The summer 1965 timetable showed only two calls at Kipling Cotes in each direction on most weekdays, but three on Wednesday and Saturday (Beverley's market days). It had the fewest stopping trains of all the remaining stations on the route, and was the only one to have been de-staffed.

On 27 January 1964 Kipling Cotes ceased to handle goods traffic, and the last train ran on Saturday 27 November 1965, the 21.42 DMU from York to Hull. Despite the snow the train was packed with enthusiasts and local people. The line officially closed on 29 November but, unlike many that were lost in the 1960s, the route was 'mothballed' for four years. The closure caused bad feeling, particularly when doubt was cast on the loss made by the service; at the public enquiry BR had assessed losses as £11,000 – a reduction on previous figures owing to dieselisation and improved working – yet the Ministry spoke of £100,000 losses. A critic suggested that this could simply have been a typing error.

Kipling Cotes: Looking north-west in October 1971, about two years after the rails had been removed. *John Mann*

Kipling Cotes: On a snowy 27 November 1965, the day when this photograph was taken, the final trains called here. The main building is to the right, and on the opposite platform, which was built in 1899 when the line was doubled, is a typical NER waiting shelter. *D. J. Mitchell*

Today the Hudson Way footpath and cycleway uses the Market Weighton-Beverley trackbed, and Kipling Cotes station is in good order. After closure Tessa Uttley, who managed the tea room at Market Weighton station, moved into the house at Kipling Cotes and opened a café. It has since become the premises of a furniture business, with the former goods shed used as a saleroom. If the 'Minsters Rail Campaign' has its way the York-Market Weighton-Beverley route will eventually reopen, but some building on the trackbed between York and Market Weighton provides a serious obstacle.

Top: **Kipling Cotes:** In April 1976 the station had altered little since closure. *Alan Young*

Above right: **Kipling Cotes:** This view is looking north-west in July 2014. The old goods shed is seen beyond the station building, both of which are used by a furniture business. *Mark Dyson*

Right: **Kipling Cotes:** Seen again in July 2014, half a century after it closed, the station has kept its character, despite a few alterations. *Mark Dyson*

HELMSLEY (1871)

Date opened	9 October 1871
Location	End of private drive off Station Road
Company on opening	North Eastern Railway
Date closed to passengers	2 February 1953
Date closed completely	10 August 1964
Company on closing	British Railways (North Eastern Region)
Present state	Station building is a private residence, with trackbed filled to level of down platform; signal box is restored, and north end of station site is woodland
County	Yorkshire North Riding (now North Yorkshire)
OS grid ref	SE618836

Helmsley is a delightful market town in Ryedale at the foot of the North York Moors and the Hambleton Hills. The central Market Place and ruined castle are accompanied by numerous old cottages built of mellow cream and honey-coloured stone under red pantile roofs. On the hillside above the castle is the woodland of Duncombe Park, ancestral home of the Earls of Feversham, and this family was instrumental in ensuring that Helmsley received a suitably elegant railway station.

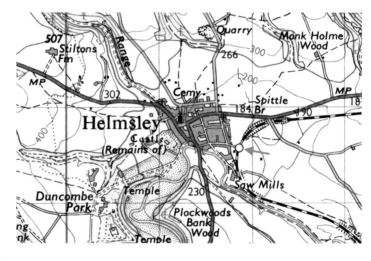

In May 1853 the Thirsk & Malton Railway opened, passing some 5 miles south of Helmsley at Gilling station. This line connected with the Malton & Driffield Junction Railway – described in the Sledmere & Fimber entry above – which opened on the same day, providing in total a single-track link of about 45 miles between what became the East Coast Main Line (at Sessay Wood Junction) and the Hull-Scarborough route. A branch to Helmsley had been part of the scheme but was abandoned. In the 1864-65 Parliamentary session two Bills that would have brought railways through Helmsley failed; however, in

1866 the NER's Gilling & Pickering route was authorised, which would provide a double-track line through Helmsley, with the existing section from the main line to Gilling upgraded to double track. The following year the NER considered abandoning the project when faced with financial uncertainties, but decided to proceed and staked out the Gilling-Helmsley section in the spring of 1869. The line officially opened to Helmsley on 9 October 1871, although a passenger train in connection with the Ryedale Agricultural Show in the town had run two months earlier.

The line to Helmsley was built as a single

track to save money, but a passing loop and two platforms were provided at the terminus, which received a 'first class station' as demanded by the Earl of Feversham, who reserved the right to scrutinise and approve the plans. The NER Architect, Thomas Prosser, adapted a standard 'villa and cross-wings' design to satisfy the Earl – Kettleness (1883) represents a less sophisticated version. Helmsley station was built of sandstone ashlar. The central two-storey villa was flanked by single-storey cross-wings that extended onto the road frontage, and a glazed entrance verandah stretched between them. The cross-wings encroached only a short distance onto the platform but their roof-lines continued as hipped glazed verandahs, and a further verandah was placed over the platform between them. A pair of dormer windows faced the platform and the road frontage. The Earl wanted green Westmorland slates for the roof, rather than standard NER blue Welsh slate, but a compromise was reached with green slates relieved by courses of scallop-edged Welsh slate. The main building was on the down (west) platform; the up platform had an unpretentious

timber shed with a hipped roof. The station was gas-lit from the outset.

This 'first class station' had lavish provision of waiting rooms: the main building contained a 1st and 2nd Class room each for ladies and gentlemen, and one for everyone else, and there was a further general waiting shed on the up platform. Supply exceeded demand, and four of the rooms were later converted into two small flats. Living accommodation for the stationmaster and his family was generous, including four large bedrooms and, eventually, a bathroom. Goods facilities included five main sidings, a stone-built warehouse, a coal depot, carriage and cattle docks, a stable, a

Helmsley: Seen looking south circa 1900, the handsome building on the right was designed to satisfy the local landowner, the Earl of Feversham of Duncombe Park. *Patrick Howat collection*

weighbridge and a weigh office. The original 11-lever signal box was at the south-west end of the down platform; a 25-lever box, a few feet beyond the platform, replaced it in 1907.

Because Helmsley is 'tucked into a corner where the Moors meet the Hambleton Hills' (Howat, 2004), to serve the town the Gilling-Pickering railway swung sharply west, with the station on the town's eastern edge. To extend beyond the temporary terminus, Helmsley to Pickering contracts were let in the summer of 1871, and the single-track route opened

Helmsley: On 1 October 1963, the final day of the five-day SLS/RCTS 'North Eastern Rail Tour', the train passes through Helmsley, hauled by 'B1' 4-6-0 No 61021. By this time the station had been closed to passengers for more than ten years and the building had lost its glazed verandah. *D. J. Mitchell*

to Kirbymoorside on 1 January 1874. Shortly before this date, work started on the final section into Pickering, which opened on 1 April 1875.

The rural surroundings of the line offered

Helmsley: The last excursion, a Sunday School special to Scarborough, calls at the station on 27 July 1964. The line and station closed to all traffic a fortnight later. *Patrick Howat*

Helmsley: The station building is seen from the forecourt in April 1976. *Alan Young*

limited passenger traffic and did not warrant a frequent service. In 1911 Helmsley station served 2,926 people, about half in the town itself, and only Kirbymoorside, with 3,538 within its catchment, exceeded the population of Helmsley in the 44 miles by rail from York to Pickering. In 1911 Helmsley station issued 14,934 tickets. In most years it was the principal station on the line for goods traffic, handling timber, barley and livestock in particular. The timber traffic was provided by Duncombe Park. In 1918, towards the end of the First World War, when a timber shortage was a national emergency, a siding about 3 miles in length was laid from Helmsley into the park for the removal of timber, and exchange sidings were built at the station on the edge of the goods yard. Duncombe siding ceased to be used in the 1930s.

In the summer of 1896 Helmsley's passenger service consisted of five down departures (towards Pickering) on weekdays, with one extra on Thursday, and the same frequency of up trains; no trains ran on Sundays. In the summer 1922 and winter 1937-38 timetables there were four in each direction. By this time passenger numbers had declined

sharply; 18,061 tickets were issued at Helmsley in 1920, falling to 8,791 in 1927 and 5,979 in 1938. Traffic dwindled on the Gilling-Malton line to such a degree that its passenger trains were withdrawn on 1 January 1931.

During the Second World War the service through Helmsley was reduced to two departures in each direction. Interwar competition from buses was keen, as the distance by road from Helmsley to York was just over 20 miles but almost 32 by rail, and by the late 1940s the railway stood no chance as 'Reliance' buses between Helmsley and York and 'United' linking Helmsley, Kirbymoorside and Pickering offered a more convenient service. The BR summer 1952 timetable showed only 7.37am and 6.10pm departures from Helmsley to York on weekdays, with an additional Saturday train at 10.41am; trains left for Pickering at 8.39am and 7.14pm, and also at 11.44am on Saturday. An unadvertised afternoon train from Pickering ran to Helmsley for schoolchildren.

In June 1950 Ampleforth station, between Helmsley and York, closed. On several routes in the early 1950s BR (NE) closed one station, followed soon by closure of the whole line, and rumours in the autumn of 1952 that the York-Gilling-Helmsley-Pickering railway was to close proved correct. The last passenger trains ran on Saturday 31 January and, although it was a particularly stormy day, people lined the platforms to witness their passing. Official closure was on 2 February, and Kirbymoorside-Pickering also closed to goods traffic on that day.

Although regular passenger trains had ceased, Helmsley and some of the other stations still saw occasional services. Gilling continued to serve as the station for Ampleforth College, and school specials called until April 1964. *The Railway Magazine* (February 1955) reported that 'restoration of special passenger train facilities' for excursions was to be granted 'at the request of people living along the branch' to enable them to visit York and Leeds for shopping and football matches. Desmond Lee, the enterprising porter/signalman at Helmsley, organised annual excursions from the mid-1950s, to various destinations including Largs and Llandudno. Howat notes that a June 1963 excursion to Kings Lynn did not return to Helmsley until 1.00am, and three gas lamps on the platform were coaxed into life to enable passengers to alight safely. Several enthusiasts' specials visited the line after passenger closure, as did ramblers' excursions, the last being the 'Daffodil and Primrose Diesel Excursion' on 3 May 1964. The connection between the main line and the route to Helmsley and Kirbymoorside was severed on 19 March 1963 when a parcels train was derailed at Sessay Wood Junction, but goods and occasional passenger trains could still travel from Helmsley to Gilling and reverse to reach Malton and the rest of the network. However, traffic was insufficient to keep the route open and complete closure was announced for 10 August 1964. On Monday 27 July the last passenger train ran from Helmsley to Scarborough and back, chartered by the town's Sunday Schools. The final pick-up goods train called on Friday 7 August. Track-lifting began at Kirbymoorside on 29 March 1965 and demolition reached Gilling in mid-June.

The sturdy station buildings on the 'Ryedale' network have largely survived, and that at Helmsley is now a private residence that retains much of its character although, regrettably, the glazed verandahs disappeared long ago.

Helmsley: This is the view across the lawn in September 2008, where there were formerly railway tracks. The station building is beautifully presented, and the signal box is still in place, partly obscured by the tree on the left. *Nick Catford*

AYSGARTH (1877)

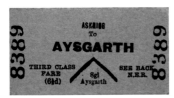

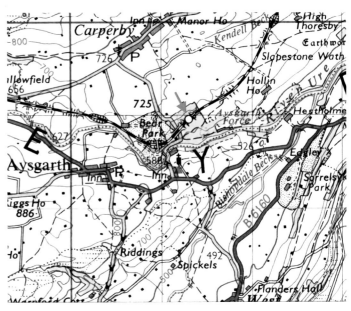

Date opened	1 February 1877
Location	East of lane leading north from Yore Bridge
Company on opening	North Eastern Railway
Date closed to passengers	26 April 1954
Date closed completely	27 April 1964
Company on closing	British Railways (North Eastern Region)
Present state	Platforms and range of buildings well preserved and undergoing restoration. Station building offers holiday accommodation
County	Yorkshire North Riding (now North Yorkshire)
OS grid ref	SE013889

While most disused stations have disappeared or have been greatly altered – and have lost much of their appeal – Aysgarth has survived, more than half a century since it closed completely, and retains a wonderful array of original features; moreover it is undergoing sensitive restoration with a view to being reopened by the Wensleydale Railway. The station was on the 39¾-mile line between Northallerton, on the East Coast Main Line, and Garsdale (known as Hawes Junction until 1932) on the celebrated Settle & Carlisle route. Aysgarth is a village of fewer than 300 inhabitants, but it is well known for the nearby waterfalls, visitors to which used the station.

For much of its length this delightful rural line followed the valley of the River Ure; this valley has been known since at least the 12th century as Wensleydale, taking its name from a village served by the railway, rather than

Aysgarth: After closure to regular passenger trains there were numerous excursions on the scenic route through Wensleydale. This passenger train is seen at Aysgarth circa 1957. *Martin Bairstow collection*

its river. The line developed in a disjointed fashion involving four separate companies. The eastern end from Northallerton to Leeming Bar (then called Leeming Lane) was authorised on 26 June 1846 and opened on 6 March 1848 by the company latterly known as the York, Newcastle & Berwick Railway, as an offshoot of the main line. The intention was to go 1¾ miles further to Bedale, but it was left to a nominally independent company, the Bedale & Leyburn Railway (B&LR) both to complete this section and to extend to Leyburn, as enabled by an Act of 4 August 1853. The line opened to Bedale on 1 February 1855 and Leyburn on 19 May 1856. From its opening the line was worked by the NER, which absorbed the B&LR in 1858. Aysgarth was now less than 8 miles from a station, but would have to wait almost two decades to be served by rail.

In the 1860s the NER was perturbed by projects for new railways in Wensleydale that would trespass into its empire. One was the Hawes & Melmerby Railway, which would pass through Leyburn en route to Melmerby (near Ripon); this received Royal Assent on 5 July 1865. The other, the North of England

Union Railway (NEUR), would run from near Settle through Garsdale, Hawes and Leyburn, then on towards Darlington. At this time the Midland Railway was pursuing the project that would ultimately become the Settle & Carlisle line (opened in 1876). An understanding was reached with the NER whereby the Midland took over the NEUR but abandoned the plans for the line east of Hawes, while the NER would build from Hawes to Leyburn and Melmerby: the NER had already invested in the Hawes & Melmerby project and had four representatives on its board. The Leyburn-Melmerby section was not proceeded with, but the NER constructed the line from Leyburn through Aysgarth to Hawes. The route was not difficult, although many cuttings and embankments were required. Unfortunately the Midland Railway, which was building the joint Midland/NER Hawes station, made slow progress, and the NER had to be content with opening only to Askrigg on 1 February 1877; trains through Hawes to Hawes Junction ran from 1 October 1878. The line was single but with passing loops at several stations, including Aysgarth, where there were two facing platforms.

A legacy of the involvement of different companies in building the line was the variety of station architecture. As an example, Hawes received a single-storey twin-pavilion structure that has numerous close relatives on the Midland's Settle & Carlisle route, from which the Hawes line was a branch, and at Addingham (described in *Lost Stations of Yorkshire: The West Riding*). Aysgarth, on the other hand, is of a style favoured by the NER when Prosser was company architect. The station building on the up (north-west) platform has a T-shaped two-storey station house under a pitched roof, to which is attached a single-storey section, also of T-shape, which contained offices and waiting facilities. An open sheltered waiting area on the platform was formerly provided between the projecting single- and double-storey gables. As seen on many NER station buildings of this era, the single-storey projection has a square bay window with its own small gable, which, like the main gables, is embellished with frilly bargeboards. The building is of uncoursed stone with ashlar quoins, and the windows and doors have dressed stone architraves. On the opposite platform is a stone-built waiting room block, of generous size, its pent roof sloping down at the front; it is accompanied, towards the north-eastern end of the platform, by a low, stone-built signal box (which had 20 levers) with a pitched roof.

Sidings were provided at Aysgarth on the up side of the line at both ends of the station. The goods yard was to the north-east with a substantial stone-built single-road shed that admirably complements the character of the station building. It survives and retains its awning and loading dock. In 1913 the principal traffic here was flour/bran and livestock. A 2-ton crane was installed. The coal yard was south-west of the station, and the weighbridge manager's office – another attractive stone building – is extant.

The NER provided the passenger service, which included the 5¾-mile Midland section between Hawes and Hawes Junction. The July 1896 timetable shows four westbound departures from Aysgarth on weekdays to Hawes Junction, and one more to

Hawes. Eastbound, to Northallerton, there were five departures, together with one at 7.18am on Mondays only. The April 1910 timetable had a more generous service of five down and six up trains on weekdays, with one up departure on Sunday. In June 1920 the timetable shows a reduction to four departures in each direction, on weekdays only. During the LNER era a similar train frequency was maintained. Special trains regularly visited the Wensleydale line during NER and LNER days, outbound to

resorts such as Morecambe, Scarborough and Saltburn, and inbound from cities including York, Leeds and Bradford for visitors to enjoy the scenery of the dale. In the mid-1930s the LNER placed camping coaches at Aysgarth, Askrigg and Wensley stations, offering inexpensive holidays for up to six people at £2 10s rent per week in high summer.

At nationalisation in January 1948 the Wensleydale line was allocated to the North Eastern Region, at first as far as Hawes

then, from the following September, to a point just short of Garsdale. In early 1953 BR announced that the passenger service between Northallerton and Garsdale would be withdrawn; a spokesman claimed that only 2½% of the local community used the line and that the closure would save up to £14,500 a year. By that time Aysgarth had three westbound departures on Monday to Friday (four on Saturday), one of which ran only as far as Hawes; eastbound there were three on Monday to Friday and four on Saturday, all running to Northallerton. The single Sunday train did a return trip between Northallerton and Leyburn. Despite vigorous protests, BR announced a closure date of 29 March 1954 (for all but the Garsdale-Hawes section), which had to be postponed until 26 April as

Aysgarth: The 'North Yorkshireman Rail Tour' calls at the station on 25 April 1964, hauled by 'B16/2' 4-6-0 No 61435, on its way to Hawes. *D. J. Mitchell*

Aysgarth: Looking north-east in April 1979. *Alan Young*

arrangements for replacement buses were incomplete. Trains on the final weekend (24-25 April) attracted many passengers, as well as sightseers on the stations.

After closure, goods services were maintained on the line, and excursions and special workings for Aysgarth School (near Jervaulx station) continued. For several years one afternoon return passenger train operated by the London Midland Region was advertised between Garsdale and Hawes, enabling railway families in Garsdale, and residents served by stations to the south, to do some brisk shopping in Hawes. The train actually ran from Bradford and back to Hellifield, but was not advertised as a through train as it had to reverse twice at Garsdale to use the Hawes bay platform.

This solitary train was withdrawn on 16 March 1959, and that stretch of line was abandoned. At the time that Northallerton-Hawes closed a promise was made that, in emergency, passenger trains would be laid on. In early January 1962 a blizzard disrupted road traffic in Wensleydale so a hastily arranged steam-hauled passenger service was provided, and Aysgarth station was one of those at which the trains called. Aysgarth continued to handle goods traffic until 27 April 1964, when the Hawes to Redmire section closed, and the rails were soon removed.

The limestone quarry at Redmire kept the 22-mile branch from the East Coast Main Line in business carrying stone to the Teesside steel complex. A pick-up goods service to Redmire calling at Bedale and Leyburn ran as required until it was withdrawn on 31 May 1982.

Aysgarth: Looking south-west in November 2009. The wonderfully preserved station awaits the extension of the Wensleydale Railway, which owns the site. *Alan Young*

Occasional excursions also visited the line. In 1992 British Steel announced that stone traffic from Redmire would in future be conveyed by road. The Wensleydale Railway Association was formed in 1990 with the aim of restoring passenger services on the route and, when the stone train ceased to run and British Rail decided to sell the line, the WRA resolved to take a proactive role and provide passenger services itself. The Ministry of Defence also had an interest in the route to carry armoured vehicles to and from Catterick Garrison. It paid for repairs and restoration of the track and the

installation of loading facilities at Redmire and did not object to the WRA taking over the line. In 2000 the WRA formed a separate operating company, Wensleydale Railway plc, to which Railtrack agreed to lease the Northallerton-Redmire line. On 4 July 2003 passenger services began between Leeming Bar and Leyburn and were extended to Redmire in August 2004. At the time of writing trains are expected soon to be extended eastwards to a temporary Northallerton (West) station. Many years ago the west-to-south curve at the junction with the main line at Northallerton was removed,

Aysgarth: The goods shed is seen in November 2009, its stone construction complementing the other buildings at the station. *Alan Young*

so direct access to Northallerton from the branch has not been possible. The WRA intends eventually to reinstate the entire route from Redmire, through Aysgarth, to Garsdale, and Wensleydale Railway plc now owns the 3-acre site of Aysgarth station. When the tracks are laid here it will undoubtedly be one of Britain's finest restored stations – a 'lost station' no more.

Aysgarth: The frontage of the station building, also in November 2009. *Alan Young*

KETTLENESS (1883)

Date opened	3 December 1883
Location	West side of unnamed minor road
Company on opening	North Eastern Railway
Date closed to passengers	5 May 1958
Date closed completely	5 May 1958
Company on closing	British Railways (North Eastern Region)
Present state	Station building used by East Cleveland Scout District as 'Seeonee Lair' campsite and activity centre; platforms survive
County	Yorkshire North Riding (now North Yorkshire)
OS grid ref	NZ832155

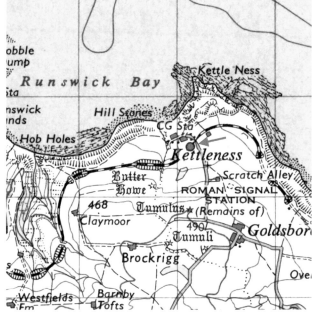

Victorian railway companies surely realised that some of their stations could never be profitable. Kettleness station was in this category, perched above 300-foot cliffs on an almost uninhabited headland. Where the North York Moors meet the coast there are some of England's highest cliffs, reaching 666 feet at Boulby, and early in the 19th century alum was quarried just north of the station site, and jet and ironstone had been worked at the foot of the cliffs. For a short time, between 1910 and 1915, an ironstone mine operated three-quarters of a mile west of the station, linked by a siding to the Loftus to Whitby line on which Kettleness was located.

The fishing port of Whitby, some 5 miles south-east of Kettleness, was reached by a railway from Pickering in 1836 – the route followed for much of its length by the preserved North Yorkshire Moors Railway, and described in the Beckhole section. To the north-west a complex network of lines developed between the Tees estuary and the Cleveland Hills – the northern edge of the Moors – to convey ironstone from the hills to the burgeoning iron industry of Middlesbrough. The small towns of Redcar and Guisborough were reached by these lines, their passenger services commencing in

1846 and 1854 respectively, and Saltburn was added to the network in 1861 as part of an attempt to create a genteel coastal resort. In April 1875 passenger trains reached the village of Loftus, which could be approached either via Guisborough or Saltburn, but in each case involving a reversal en route as these towns' stations were left stranded on branches when lines were extended beyond them.

The Whitby, Redcar & Middlesbrough Union

Kettleness: The down (north-west) platform is seen in the early 20th century. The station building was a standard NER design that was probably larger than Kettleness needed and looked out of place in its picturesque rural setting. *John Mann collection*

Railway (WR&MUR) was incorporated in July 1866 to build the route from Loftus to Whitby, through Kettleness. The contract to build the line was eventually signed in May 1871 with John Dickson, who began work by the end of the month, but his financial embarrassment halted the work in 1874. At the request of the WR&MUR, on 1 July 1875 the NER took a perpetual lease on the company and appointed John Waddell as contractor to complete the line by 13 July 1881. Unfortunately the previous contractor's work was found wanting; indeed, a section of the trackbed on the cliff edge between Sandsend and Kettleness had already collapsed into the sea, so the line was re-routed inland. Two tunnels were required, at Sandsend (1,652 yards) and Kettleness (308 yards). Deep ravines had to be crossed, and distinctive tubular steel viaducts strode over them. Of the five, the 17-span structure at Staithes, 263

yards in length and 152 feet high, was the most spectacular.

The single-track line from Loftus to Whitby (Town) opened on 3 December 1883, and was about 17 miles in length. Kettleness was one of the stations provided with two platforms to enable trains to pass. In the 1860s, when Thomas Prosser was its architect (1854-74), the NER developed a style of station building that, with a number of variations, continued to be used into the 1880s; one variation has already been encountered at Aysgarth. The version at Kettleness and the other wayside stations between Whitby (West Cliff) and Loftus was of generous proportions, but the sprawling, red-brick structure looked utterly out of place in its rural setting. Biddle (1973) notes that this 'dull, but substantial villa-type standard station could have been transplanted from any Victorian middle-class suburb.' Placed on the down (north-west) platform at Kettleness, its centrepiece was a two-storey house under a pitched slate roof aligned with the platform, with single-storey wings at each end; these were L-shaped with a gable facing the platform and a hipped roof parallel to the platform.

Three hefty chimneystacks crowned the roof of the villa, with one on each of the wings. A verandah was clasped between the wings. Door and window openings had segmental arches, and modest decoration was provided with inconspicuous blue brick courses. In contrast to the vast amount of brick on the down platform, the north-east end of the up platform had a tall stone wall where it backed onto the coal drops, and attached to it was a neat open-fronted timber waiting shed with a pent roof and indented valance. South-east of the up platform the goods facilities consisted of a siding-with-loop serving the coal drops and two further sidings to the cattle dock. A further siding was located on the down side, north east of the level crossing. The signal box, decorated with frilly bargeboards, was on the up platform, west of the station building.

On 16 July 1885 the railway from Whitby to Scarborough opened. (Ravenscar, also on this line, is the subject of the next entry.) It continued directly from the Middlesbrough-Loftus-Whitby (West Cliff) route, so trains could now run between Middlesbrough and Scarborough through Kettleness. These bypassed Whitby (Town), but shuttle services were provided between the two stations.

Kettleness: On 23 April 1957 a southbound passenger train hauled by 'L1' No 67764 calls at the station. *Les Turnbull*

The July 1896 NER timetable shows six down trains to Whitby West Cliff on weekdays, four continuing to Scarborough – these trains would be described as 'up' trains beyond West Cliff – and six up trains to Saltburn. The June 1920 service was five trains on Monday to Friday (six on Saturday) in each direction. In both 1896 and 1920 all trains called at Kettleness, and there was no service on Sunday.

NER statistics for 1911 indicate the limited use of Kettleness, with only 94 people within its catchment area and 6,574 tickets issued. In 1913 the station handled 2,595 tons of iron ore presumably from the short-lived mine to the west, and 26 wagons of livestock.

Bairstow (2008) points out that Kettleness was one of the first stations to benefit from the LNER experiment with camping coaches in the summer of 1933. Initial publicity advised that one was for hire on the Loftus-Whitby line, that it could be booked at Sandsend, Kettleness or Staithes, and, on request to the stationmaster, that it could be moved to a different station on this line during the course of the holiday.

Kettleness: The down platform is seen here on 22 March 1958. *G. C. Lewthwaite*

Campers were warned that some stations – such as Kettleness – were remote from shops and other amenities, but that the stationmaster, their 'best friend', would buy in provisions by prior arrangement. The experiment proved successful and by 1938 two camping coaches were available at Kettleness. That summer ten down trains on weekdays and seven on Sundays called at Kettleness, with 11 weekday and six Sunday trains in the opposite direction. Some trains no longer called at Kettleness.

By the summer of 1952 trains were less frequent, again some running fast through Kettleness. However, the express 8.26am departure from Middlesbrough to Scarborough called only at Staithes, Kettleness and Whitby (West Cliff), the Kettleness stop being to pass a northbound train. The winter 1957-58 timetable shows a sparse service of three departures each way on weekdays only. In September 1957 BR announced its intention of closing the Loftus-Whitby (West Cliff)

line to all traffic. Between the two places no major centres of population were served, and there was an alternative route between Middlesbrough and Whitby via Battersby. This route, too, served no centres of importance, but enabled children in the Esk Valley, with its inadequate road system, to travel to school in Whitby. BR estimated that closure from Loftus to Whitby would allow annual savings of £10,950 in operating costs and avoid £57,000 of essential structural maintenance over five years on tunnels and viaducts.

The final trains ran on Saturday 3 May 1958. An eloquent chapter is written by Stuart

Kettleness: On Saturday 3 May 1958, the final day of passenger services between Loftus and Whitby, the final trains cross at Kettleness – the 5.37pm to Whitby Town (right) and the 5.38pm to Middlesbrough. *Jim Lake collection*

Kettleness: Since the mid-1960s the old station has been used as a scout activity centre and campsite. Some activity is seen in front of the station building on 7 April 1980. *Alan Young*

Carmichael in Bairstow's *Railways around Whitby* Vol 1 (2008) of his arrival by train at Sandsend, the next station south from Kettleness, on this last day to stay in the camping coach; the curious void in the train-less week that followed; and having to depart by bus. On Monday 5 May diesel multiple units took over the Middlesbrough-Whitby-Scarborough and Loftus branch services, and from the following April Malton-Whitby services were also diesel-operated. The goods facilities at Kettleness operated until the date of passenger closure. In 1959 the tracks were lifted and the viaducts, which provided a large quantity of scrap

metal, were dismantled in 1960. On 2 May 1960 Loftus station closed to passengers and the branch was cut back to Guisborough, while Whitby (West Cliff) lasted until 12 June 1961. After closure, the ample proportions of the station building at Kettleness and its remote location attracted the interest of East Cleveland Scout District, which leased the station from the estate of the Marquis of Normanby in 1963 and opened it as an activity centre and campsite the following year. Externally the station has retained its character and is well worth a visit.

Kettleness: Looking north-east in March 2002, the leaning tree in the background is a reminder that the station is close to a windswept cliff top. *Alan Young*

RAVENSCAR (1885)

Date opened	16 July 1885
Location	South side of Station Square
Company on opening	Scarborough & Whitby Railway
Date closed to passengers	8 March 1965
Date closed completely	8 March 1965
Company on closing	British Rail (North Eastern Region)
Present state	Buildings demolished, but up platform and base of down platform waiting shelter survive
County	Yorkshire North Riding (now North Yorkshire)
OS grid ref	NZ985013

The headland at Peak, midway between Whitby and Scarborough, is flanked by cliffs rising to 600 feet. In 1640 alum, a mineral used in the textile and medicinal trades, was discovered in the lias shales at the cliff top, and for two centuries a quarry and processing plant operated here. The product was exported by sea from a dock at the foot of the cliff, and at times when its market value was high there were raids by Dutch, French and Spanish pirates, requiring a cannon to be placed on the cliff top to ward them off. By the time the railway arrived in 1885 the industry had faded, but there were soon very ambitious development plans for Peak – which would be renamed Ravenscar.

In July 1865 an Act was passed authorising the construction of the Scarborough & Whitby Railway (S&WR). The NER responded to this threat of competition within its territory by opening a north-to-east curve at Rillington to provide its own service between the two towns, but this route was 56 miles long, while Scarborough and Whitby were only 20 miles apart. No progress was made by the S&WR, and the NER withdrew its service. In June 1871 a new S&WR Act was passed for a realigned route, isolated from existing lines,

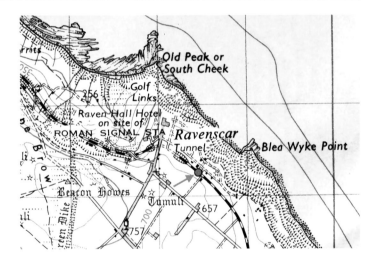

which included a 1 in 5½ incline at the Whitby end. However, an Act of May 1873 allowed for connections to the NER at each end, but with little progress made apart from some work at the Scarborough end a fresh Act of 1880 was required to revive the project. The NER agreed to work the line in return for half the receipts and it opened on 16 July 1885. To reach

both of the termini a reversal was required, at
Prospect Hill Junction (Whitby) and Falsgrave
Junction (Scarborough). The splendid 13-arch
Larpool Viaduct was constructed to carry
the line across the Esk Valley just south of
Whitby. The single-track line meandered on
its way as it followed the easiest route close
to the cliff-lined coast, but severe gradients
were still required, particularly gruesome ones
approaching Peak, the aptly named 631-foot
summit of the line, with two miles at 1 in 41
from the south and 2½ miles at 1 in 39 from
the north; this latter stretch also included a
curved 279-yard tunnel close to the summit,
built at the insistence of the owner of nearby
Raven Hall, W. H. Hammond, who preferred not
to have his view disfigured by the S&WR, even
though he was one of its directors. The gradient
was enough of a problem for southbound
trains, especially when coastal 'sea fret' fogs
caused locomotives to slip on the track, but
the unnecessary tunnel was particularly wet
and locos sometimes slid to a halt in it. On
occasions trains had to 'set back' and have

Ravenscar: The station is seen looking north-west
circa 1907, before the second platform was built.
The modest timber building would prove adequate
because plans to develop a holiday resort here
produced little else but the parade of shops on the
right and a few scattered houses. *Alan Young collection*

another attempt to reach Peak – sometimes
as many as five attempts were required. Peak
station was on the short, near-level section on
the summit, the topography determining its
location rather than its convenience of access
to the few habitations. The single platform on
the up (seaward) side was provided with a small
timber building, and there was a short siding
immediately north-west of the platform.

The NER took issue with the S&WR for
failing to provide a house for the stationmaster
and threatened that its trains would no longer
call at Peak unless one was built. The smaller
company took no action, so trains ceased to
stop on 6 March 1895, calling again from 1
August 1896 when the matter was resolved.
The NER bought the line in August 1898 for
less than half what it had cost to build.

When Hammond died in 1895 his home,
Raven Hall, and its estate were bought by the
Ravenscar Estate Co Ltd with the intention of
creating a holiday resort on the 750 acres. The
name 'Ravenscar' was adopted as a marketing
ploy; Raven Hall provided the first element,
to which the Yorkshire suffix 'scar', meaning
a cliff, was added. The S&WR obligingly gave
this name to Peak station on 1 October 1897.
Work on the resort was soon under way. Its
roads (already named) and drains were laid out,
and a zigzag path from the projected Marine
Esplanade to the Hanging Gardens of Ravenscar

Ravenscar: BR Standard 2-6-4T No 80117 draws a southbound passenger train into the station on 24 April 1957. *Les Turnbull*

Ravenscar: Looking south-east from the up platform circa 1960. The down platform, added with the passing loop in 1908, has an enclosed pent-roof timber shelter, a typical NER feature, as are the cradle-mounted oil lanterns and the 'diagonal' fencing. The short terrace in the background was one of the few buildings constructed in 'the town that never was'. *G. C. Lewthwaite*

was constructed. Raven Hall was extended and converted into a hotel. Special trains ran from cities in the West Riding and Midlands to bring potential purchasers of plots to view the splendours of the site, with fares refunded to those who decided to buy. Ravenscar offered a vista of incontestable magnificence over Robin Hood's Bay, the air was bracing – a feature much prized by Victorians – and a golf course was laid out, but the location had serious shortcomings. The north-facing promontory was frequently blasted by cold winds or swathed in fog, while the shoreline, 600 feet below, consisted of rock platforms and little beach. To reach the resort, visitors would have to travel through the established resorts of Scarborough or Whitby (both with excellent

Ravenscar: A southbound DMU calls at the station in early 1965, shortly before the line closed. The solitary Edwardian parade of shops is in the background. *Jim Lake collection*

beaches), then, as already mentioned, rail access to Ravenscar was single-track and heavily graded, presenting the railway operator with considerable problems.

The Ravenscar Estate Company prospectus confidently announced that 'it needs little prescience to foresee that the future of Ravenscar as a watering place is practically assured.' However, when the 1,500 plots came up for auction in 1900 there was little interest,

and development was limited to a distinctly urban block of four buildings in the fashionable domestic revival style on the square adjoining the station, and a few scattered houses on the broad new thoroughfares. Optimism had clearly not evaporated in 1908 when Ravenscar station received a passing loop and a second platform of timber (with a small waiting shed) to enable more trains and passengers to be handled. Very short sidings were also added north-west of the down platform and south-

Ravenscar: Looking south-east towards the up platform in April 1974. *Alan Young*

Ravenscar: The up platform looking north-west in May 2007. *Neil Cholmondeley*

east of the up platform. However, in 1911 the local population of only 230 and a meagre 4,860 tickets issued – fewer than at Kettleness, which had no pretensions to being a holiday resort – revealed the degree to which the planned town had failed. Before the First World War Ravenscar Estate became bankrupt and the resort progressed no further.

One modest success was the establishment of the Whitaker brickworks within the old alum quarry in 1900, reached by a siding from the railway. Although intended to supply the materials for the town of Ravenscar, the kilns went on to produce bricks for a housing estate and the Odeon cinema in Scarborough.

The July 1896 NER timetable shows six train departures from Peak each way on weekdays, and one more on Thursday, despite – as noted above – no trains actually calling until August. Timetables for April 1910, June 1920 and September 1937 all show five weekday departures each way from Ravenscar. Summers in the 1930s brought much tourist traffic to the line, encouraged by attractive fares, and in July 1938 there were 12 departures each way on weekdays with one more on Monday

and Thursday, and 14 southbound and 16 northbound trains on Saturday; even on Sunday there were nine trains each way. By that date Ravenscar boasted two camping coaches. During the Second World War the services were significantly reduced, with four weekday trains each way in July 1943, but the summer 1952 timetable shows a return to something approaching pre-war frequency, including Sunday trains.

During the 1950s cost-cutting measures were applied to the Whitby-Scarborough line. In March 1953 Scalby station closed; this had served the largest settlement along the line, and in 1911 had been the busiest intermediate station, but buses drained passengers away from what was almost a suburb of Scarborough. Hayburn Wyke was de-staffed in March 1955 and Fyling Hall in May 1958, but Ravenscar retained its staff until the end. In BR days Ravenscar station was little changed from Edwardian times, but on 5 May 1958 diesel multiple units appeared, replacing steam on the Middlesbrough-Battersby-Whitby-Scarborough service; this was the day when trains through Ravenscar ceased to use the Loftus-Whitby route via Kettleness, as described in the previous section. In March 1963 the Beeching Report dealt savagely with the North York

Moors and coast, recommending closure of all three routes to Whitby, and formal notice was published on 14 February 1964. From 4 May Ravenscar closed to goods traffic. On 11 September Ernest Marples, Secretary of State for Transport, refused permission to close the Whitby-Battersby-Middlesbrough line, but consented to the withdrawal of services to Malton and Scarborough. Despite a long and bitter fight, and recognition that closure of the line through Ravenscar would cause 'serious hardship', both lines closed completely on Monday 8 March 1965. Two days earlier, the final day when trains ran, the line attracted many visitors, and the steam-hauled 'Whitby Moors Railtour' from Manchester ran from Scarborough to Whitby before taking the line through Pickering to Malton. A railway preservation group considered purchasing the Whitby-Scarborough line to operate it as the 'Yorkshire Coast Railway', but the cost proved excessive. In 1967 five local authorities combined to examine the practicality of reopening the line using a rate subsidy, and BR actually suggested a timetable of four return trains per day, but the councils' enthusiasm waned when an estimated annual loss of £23,000 was forecast. Early in 1968 track-lifting began, with a stretch of line from Hawsker to Whitby temporarily spared as the possibility of potash mining close to the route was being investigated. The 'Yorkshire Coast Railway' preservation group transferred its attention to the Whitby-Malton route, as far as Pickering, which now thrives as the North Yorkshire Moors Railway.

By 1974 Ravenscar station's timber buildings had disappeared, but the up platform still had its lamp posts, oil lantern cradles and nameboard stanchions. Today the platform is still in place, and the trackbed is a bridleway known as the 'Scarborough to Whitby Rail Trail' or 'Scarborough to Whitby Cinder Track'. The historical interest of Ravenscar prompted the National Trust to acquire the old alum and brick works and the cliff-top area, and it operates a visitor centre. Raven Hall is still a hotel, and there is a café in the Edwardian 'town centre' buildings in Station Square. Exploration of the 'town that never was' is highly recommended.

South Cave: Looking south-west from Kettlethorpe Hill bridge, two coal trains pass on an unknown date. Both the main building on the up platform (left) and the down platform shelter have generously sized awnings. A long siding is seen behind the down platform, but the main goods facilities are on the up side beyond the passenger station. *Jim Lake collection*

More than a mile north of the village of South Cave, the A1034 passes the unmistakeable site of an old station whose building looks as if it belongs in a town rather than in this quiet countryside. East of the station the former Hull & Barnsley Railway (H&BR) line headed into the lonely Wolds,

SOUTH CAVE (1885)

Date opened	22 July 1885
Location	West side of Kettlethorpe Hill (A1034)
Company on opening	Hull, Barnsley & West Riding Junction Railway & Dock Company (Hull & Barnsley Railway)
Date closed to passengers	1 August 1955
Date closed completely	6 April 1959
Company on closing	British Railways (North Eastern Region)
Present state	Station building/stationmaster's house in commercial use, and platforms removed
County	Yorkshire East Riding (now East Riding of Yorkshire)
OS grid ref	SE918328

needing three tunnels and a huge cutting on its way to Hull. Yet 45 years before it was built, another line, owned by the NER, took the easy route a few miles south through the more densely populated lowland beside the River Humber; this route remains open today. Chapman (1999) explains that, 'built to compete with well-established lines, the H&B was born late in the railway building era, and as the various railway companies gradually merged into a more unified system it became less relevant and died early.'

The line was built because some influential Hull businessmen believed that their city was disadvantaged by the monopoly that the NER held over its freight transport, and the city's Corporation supported them. The group was intent on providing a new route for coal from the Barnsley area to a dock in Hull, which they also proposed to build – hence the cumbersome name by which their company was originally known, the Hull, Barnsley & West

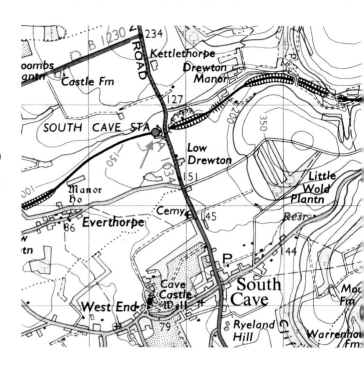

South Cave: In March 1955 a passenger train to Hull hauled by a 'G5' calls at the station, several months before closure. By this time the verandah has been removed from the main building. *J. C. W. Halliday*

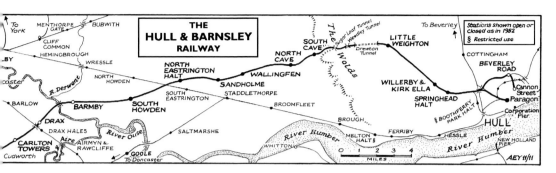

South Cave: A map of the surrounding railway network. *Alan Young*

Riding Junction Railway & Dock Company.

The Hull & Selby Railway – part of the NER from 1854 – reached Hull in 1840. It was almost level and remarkably direct, including an 18-mile straight section, the longest in Britain. In contrast, from the edge of the city trains on the H&BR faced an adverse gradient of 1 in 108 for 6 miles, and between Little Weighton and South Cave the line had an 83-foot-deep

South Cave: The H&BR did not stint itself when building South Cave and the other stations between Hull and Howden. The generous width of the up platform, from which this photograph was taken in October 1971, and the unexpectedly large building in a lightly populated area testify to the company's misjudged optimism. *John Mann*

cutting and three tunnels, at Drewton (1 mile 356 yards) and Sugar Loaf and Weedley (each 132 yards). A long stretch at 1 in 150 took the line down from the Wolds, after which it was almost level, but substantial bridges crossed the rivers Ouse and Aire. Further west the land rose, and there were further tunnels. In its favour, the H&BR passed through Howden, a town that the NER missed by 2 miles, and within Hull bridges carried the railway over roads while the NER had several busy level crossings. However, the H&BR's Cannon Street terminus in Hull was inconveniently placed to serve the city centre, and at its western end the line failed to reach Barnsley!

The cost of constructing the H&BR was twice the estimate and building work had to cease for some months when funds dried up. Despite financial pressures – or contributing

South Cave: Looking south-west in October 1971, the 'staggered' nature of the platforms is clear, the down platform displaced to the west. The goods shed is visible in the distance. *John Mann*

to them – this double-track line primarily for freight traffic was given some extravagant stations, although its humble Cannon Street terminus in Hull was intended to be a carriage shed and was 'one of the sorry band of temporary stations that became permanent' (Biddle 1973). South Cave had two facing platforms, but the northern (down) one was displaced slightly to the west. The extensive main building, grand even by H&BR standards, was on the broad south platform. Built of red brick, its two-storey stationmaster's

South Cave: A general view from the road bridge in April 1976. *Alan Young*

South Cave: The southern elevation of the station building is seen on the same date. The variety of roof lines and asymmetrical placing of gables contribute to the attraction of this structure. *John Mann*

house had a hipped roof from which pairs of gables stood forward on the platform elevation and facing the forecourt, while lofty single-storey sections continued both east and west. The western section under a pitched roof contained the office range, and it ended with a further gabled element, where the ladies' room was found. Most of the gables carried decorated bargeboards, with half-timbering added on the exterior elevation. East of the stationmaster's house the single-storey building rose up to a plain parapet. A particularly attractive feature was the awning with a decorated valance, which stretched across the broad platform. The opposite platform had a modest waiting shed but its roof was carried forward to form a verandah that complemented the awning on the up platform.

The site of South Cave station was spacious and accommodated goods facilities that handled the standard range of traffic. There were two sidings and a shed south of the running lines, and two further sidings to the north, reached from the west. A 2-ton yard crane was installed. The signal box stood directly north of the shed.

In December 1895 on weekdays up to 11

trains called at South Cave in each direction – with different frequencies and some calls by request – and two on Sunday. In July 1922 there were nine Monday-to-Friday departures, ten on Saturday and one on Sunday in each direction. Three months earlier the H&BR had become part of the NER, and from 1923 it was operated by the LNER. Following the amalgamation, the 20 'duplicated' miles of the H&BR from Hull to Eastrington, where it crossed the NER route, could have been closed if a new link from the NER to the rest of the H&BR, approved by an Act of 1923, had been built. This would have enabled the part of the route that directly served the Barnsley coalfield to be retained.

Passenger trains were particularly lightly loaded on the H&BR west of Howden, and from 1 January 1932 they were withdrawn, having already been discontinued on the Denby branch in 1903 and the Wath branch in 1929. The Howden-Cudworth closure removed passenger trains from $38\frac{1}{2}$ route miles and, as pointed out by White (1986), was 'the first closure in Britain

Above: **South Cave:** On 14 April 1987 the
station building is empty and the slates have largely
been removed. A few months later the trackbed
was infilled to platform level and the building was
renovated. *Alan Young*

Below: **South Cave:** In April 1987 the building is
about to be renovated. The 'half-timbered' near gable
and the decorated bargeboards on the distant ones
are points of interest. *Alan Young*

South Cave: In July 1990 the station building has been renovated and the former trackbed has been infilled in the foreground. The old goods depot is visible in the distance. *Mark Dyson*

of any line that could be called a main line, albeit a competing and now redundant one'. The Hull-South Howden section continued to enjoy a service provided, since 1928, by Sentinel steam railcars, though these gave way in 1941 to push-and-pull trains using adapted 'G5' 0-4-4 tank locomotives. The winter 1937-38 timetable shows nine departures from South Cave on Monday to Friday in each direction, 13 down and 14 up on Saturday, but none on Sunday. Under BR(NE) administration the passenger service in the summer of 1950 was similar to the wartime frequency, with seven trains each way on Monday to Friday and nine on Saturday, but in the winter of 1954 it had decreased to five each way on weekdays, and eight down and seven up on Saturday. By the spring of 1955 the main building had lost its awning.

Use of the Hull-South Howden trains dwindled and the service was withdrawn on 1 August 1955. The last passenger train through

South Cave was a South Howden-Bridlington excursion on 30 August 1958. Goods traffic continued along the line and at South Cave, but on 6 April 1959 the approximately 35-mile route from Little Weighton to Wrangbrook Junction was abandoned, including South Cave. Track-lifting took place through the station in June 1963. Before closure to passengers, the awnings had been removed from the buildings on both platforms, and the down platform shelter was demolished. The main building remained in place, but by the late 1980s it was derelict. In 1990, following restoration, it was in residential use and the platforms had been removed. It is now the premises of a trailer hire firm.

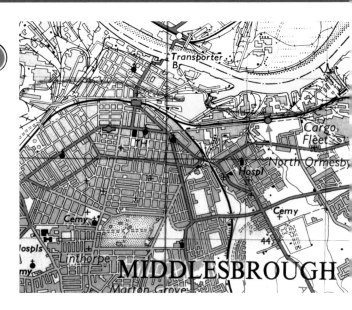

CARGO FLEET

Cargo Fleet station was a little over a mile east of Middlesbrough on the line to Redcar and Saltburn. Although now a large town of more than 140,000 inhabitants, Middlesbrough was a late arrival on Britain's urban map. For centuries Stockton was the lowest bridging point and principal port close to the mouth of the River Tees.

Date opened	8 November 1885 (although name used previously for nearby stations)
Location	On still-open Middlesbrough-Saltburn line, a mile east of Middlesbrough station, adjacent to Dockside Road, between junctions with Marsh Road and Works Road
Company on opening	North Eastern Railway
Date closed to passengers	22 January 1990
Date closed completely	22 January 1990
Company on closing	British Rail (Eastern Region)
Present state	Demolished, and Saltburn-Middlesbrough up line has been slewed through site of platform
County	Yorkshire North Riding (now Middlesbrough)
OS grid ref	NZ512205

In 1811 Middlesbrough was a hamlet of 35 inhabitants, and by 1831 the figure was still only 154. The town's foundation was prompted by the opening of the Stockton & Darlington Railway (S&DR) in 1825, the pioneering passenger and mineral line whose primary function was to carry coal from central and western County Durham to tidal water for export. Stockton was adopted as the coal port, but it was soon evident that larger facilities closer to the sea were needed. Joseph Pease, a prominent figure in the S&DR and a member of the influential Quaker banking family, persuaded the S&DR management to extend the railway eastwards from Stockton, and by 1830 it reached the new staithes close to Middlesbrough Farm (almost directly north of the present Middlesbrough station). A group of speculators purchased 527 acres for the construction of a new town to service the port,

on a site described by a contemporary reporter as 'a dismal swamp'.

From the 1840s ironworks were established close to Middlesbrough, and the discovery of ironstone in the nearby Cleveland Hills prompted the rapid expansion of the industry along the south bank of the Tees; a branch line from the Eston mines contributed traffic to the line through Cargo Fleet. By the 1920s several miles of the south bank of the Tees adjoining the Middlesbrough-Redcar line were lined with industry. After the First World War the iron,

Cargo Fleet: A westbound passenger train hauled by what appears to be a BR 2MT calls at the station in 1955. The entrance to the glazed brick subway giving access to the island platform is in the foreground. *Stations UK*

Cargo Fleet: In the early 1960s a 'J27' hauls a freight train carrying steel past the station. Cochrane's pipe works is on the left. *Raymond Trough*

Cargo Fleet: The station is seen in its industrial surroundings on 26 September 1972, looking west from a Saltburn-Darlington DMU. The BR(NE) nameboard in the region's tangerine livery is hand-painted; the gas lamps have been removed from their posts. *Alan Young*

steel and engineering works were joined by oil-refining, chemical and petrochemical factories. This busy industrial region continued to grow in the 1960s, and the author's recollection of his first train journey between Middlesbrough and Redcar in 1963 was of a tormented landscape swathed in smoke and steam, a nauseous smell of sulphur, and expanses of sidings where steam locos were hauling and shunting rakes of wagons. While de-industrialisation set in elsewhere by the 1970s, the heavy industries of Teesside battled on, but in the 1980s-90s many of the factories were abandoned. The scenes of dereliction along the railway route were as ugly as they were distressing. From the early 1990s reclamation of the derelict industrial land

began, notably the 'flagship' development on a brownfield site of the Riverside Stadium, home of Middlesbrough FC, which opened in 1995 a few hundred yards west of Cargo Fleet station.

The Middlesbrough & Redcar Railway, authorised by an Act of 21 July 1845, opened to passengers on 5 June 1846, but from the outset the line was an important goods route. The first train was hauled by *Locomotion No 1*. The line was leased to the S&DR on 1 October 1847 and formally amalgamated with that company on 30 June 1862. In turn, the NER absorbed the S&DR on 13 July 1863. At the eastern end, the original terminus at Redcar was replaced on 19 August 1861 when the line was extended to Saltburn; both towns subsequently developed into holiday resorts. Stations on this line present a challenge to railway historians, as some of their dates of opening are difficult to establish, some were probably or definitely resited, and names were changed and even exchanged between stations.

Cargo Fleet (meaning 'cold stream') had acquired a station by April 1847, as instructions have been found to provide a nameboard for 'Cleveland Port' station, and in March 1848 a platform was ordered for 'Cargo Fleet' – referring to the same location. It appeared as 'Cleveland Port' in the railway company timetables by September 1847, as it did in

Bradshaw until 1867, while company minutes generally referred to it as Cargo Fleet. Minutes of 1851 and 1865 also reveal that the station might have been resited either once or twice. In the light of this it is difficult to know whether the station that existed from 1885 until 1990 should be known as the second, third or fourth Cargo Fleet station.

On 9 November 1885 a new station opened to serve Cargo Fleet, approximately a quarter of a mile west of its predecessors. By this time the route carried huge volumes of goods and mineral traffic, and the station was an island platform within a multiple-track system; this island layout at wayside stations was largely confined in NER territory to lines that were being widened. The contract for the new Cargo Fleet station was awarded in May 1884 to W. C. Atkinson of Stockton. To reduce costs its structure included material salvaged from the Middlesbrough excursion station at Wood Street, and the eventual cost of £2,317 for the platform, buildings and verandah represented a saving of £1,600. The platform had a straight northern (down) face, but the southern face was curved. The road approach was from the west, the road running south of the passenger railway tracks. Access to the station was via a glazed brick subway that passed under the up track and emerged almost midway along the platform, at the western end of the station building. The latter was an austere, single-storey brick structure with a slated pitched roof. The booking hall was at its western end, facing the entrance to the subway, while the remainder of the building included offices and toilets. Surrounding the building was a shallow-pitched slated verandah, which was partially glazed. A frilly iron valance pierced with lines of holes added charm to the otherwise utilitarian building. Cargo Fleet was purely a passenger station, although several nearby sidings handled goods traffic. The 1904 RCH *Handbook* records sidings that served two ironworks, one with a brickworks and wharf; a warrant stores; a timber yard and wharves; and a salt works and wharf.

Cargo Fleet: The northern side of the island platform is seen from a passing train on 26 September 1972. The building still has its verandah with its unusual metal valance. The station has been unstaffed for three years and is gradually being vandalised. *Alan Young*

For much of its life Cargo Fleet had the least frequent train service of the intermediate stations between Middlesbrough and Redcar. In 1896 about half of the trains that called at the other stations stopped at Cargo Fleet. In 1920 a number of Middlesbrough-Redcar 'stopping' trains continued to miss Cargo Fleet, but the frequency increased: on Monday to Friday there were 14 down calls, 18 on Saturday and three on Sunday, and in the opposite direction 19 called on Monday to Friday, 23 on Saturday, and three on Sunday. At this time trains on the Eston branch also served Cargo Fleet, but there were only four per day (Sunday included). In the winter of 1937-38 the LNER provided an hourly service, increased in frequency during the morning and evening rush hours. In the down direction there were 24 trains on Monday to Friday, 25 on Saturday and five on Sunday, with 22 on weekdays and seven on Sunday in the opposite direction.

BR(NE) introduced DMUs on the Darlington-Middlesbrough-Saltburn services from 19 August 1957, and the following summer Cargo Fleet had a half-hourly service, with almost every train calling. On Sunday an even more intensive service was operated, reflecting the popularity of Redcar, Marske and Saltburn for day trips. It is remarkable that Sunday trains called at Cargo Fleet, since the station was poorly sited to serve residential areas. About the same time as 'dieselisation' of the train services, some modest updating of the station took place when totem name signs were installed; however, these were attached to gas lamps. The nameboards were hand-painted wooden examples rather than the vitreous enamel installed at the other stations along the line.

On 4 May 1969 the Darlington-Saltburn line was converted to 'Paytrain' operation, and Cargo Fleet was one of the many stations to be reduced to what were popularly known as 'unstaffed halts'. The removal of staff made the station attractive to vandals, and by 1972 the windows were boarded up, brickwork was daubed with graffiti, lamps were smashed, and peeling remains of posters clung to the notice boards. When these buildings were demolished the station received a small brick shelter, and electric lighting with Corporate Identity name signs was installed. By 1981 Cargo Fleet's train service had been reduced to hourly intervals with extras at rush hours, but there was still an enhanced Sunday service.

The Middlesbrough-Redcar route, by running close to the Tees, served riverside industries adequately with numerous sidings, and the wayside stations, including Cargo Fleet,

were far better placed to serve industry than residential areas. In 1911 Cargo Fleet station was estimated to have 682 people living within its catchment and 55,070 tickets were issued; since the station principally served factories, many passengers would have bought return tickets at their 'home' station, rather than at Cargo Fleet. The closure of riverside factories in the 1980s left Cargo Fleet, South Bank and Grangetown with very few passengers. At Cargo Fleet and Grangetown the use of the stations declined so much that in the late 1980s their closure was considered. BR decided that Cargo Fleet would require an outlay of £60,000 on the station structure in 1990-91 if it remained open. A traffic census found no regular users, and only three passengers on Monday to Friday, one on Saturday and five on Sunday made 'casual use' of the station. When the formal closure proposal was published there were, therefore, no objections from regular users; the two written objections were readily dismissed. Consequently on 22 January 1990 Cargo Fleet station closed – one of relatively few on the British network to be lost in the last 30 years. The derelict platform survived until at least 2002, but has now been demolished, and the up line has been repositioned on part of the platform site.

Cargo Fleet: The station is seen from a passing train on 29 May 1984. Following demolition of the Victorian building a 'bus shelter' was provided for passenger comfort, and modern lighting was installed. *Alan Young*

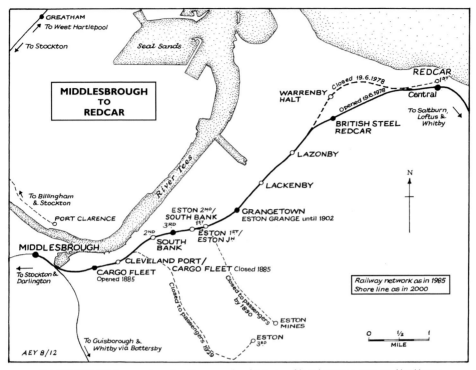

Cargo Fleet: A map showing the complex history of local station names. *Alan Young*

THORGANBY (1913)

Date opened	21 July 1913
Location	East side of Bonby Lane
Company on opening	Derwent Valley Light Railway
Date closed to passengers	1 September 1926
Date closed completely	31 December 1964
Company on closing	Derwent Valley Light Railway
Present state	Station building derelict, but stationmaster's house in residential use
County	Yorkshire East Riding (now North Yorkshire)
OS grid ref	SE678408

The Derwent Valley Light Railway was built to carry farm produce. It served an agricultural area south-east of York that lacked railway communication, and was to be affectionately known as 'the Farmers' Line' or 'the Blackberry Line'. Its passenger service was short-lived, but it continued for many years to carry agricultural goods.

In 1902 an Order was obtained by a consortium of councils in the Vale of York to build a line to serve the Derwent Valley south-east of the city, but they balked at the expected construction cost of £100,000. In 1907 a reconstituted company emerged, known as the Derwent Valley Light Railway, which eventually built a standard-gauge route from Cliff Common, adjacent to the NER station on the Selby-Market Weighton line, to a terminus at Layerthorpe, 1¼ miles north-east of York NER station, but connected to it by the Foss Islands goods branch.

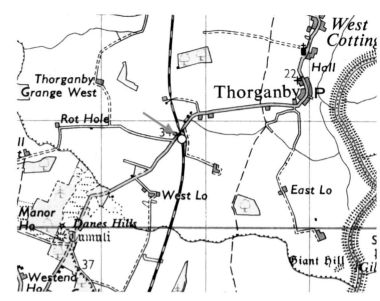

The 16-mile single-track line was built as a Light Railway under an Act of 1896, which had been intended to encourage the expansion of the network in areas not previously served and thereby promote economic development. The Act permitted such lines to be constructed relatively cheaply with lighter rails and thinner ballast than was the normal standard, unattended and ungated level crossings, minimal station facilities, an absence of lineside fencing and limited

signalling. The DVLR used second-hand Midland Railway rails, and a 25mph speed limit was observed in accordance with Light Railway Act requirements. The line opened throughout to passengers and goods on 21 July 1913, although the southern section from Cliff Common, through Thorganby, to Wheldrake had been carrying goods traffic since 29 October 1912.

Thorganby: Nearly 40 years after passenger trains ceased to call here, the station is seen in July 1964, in good repair and even sporting a DVLR style of nameboard, attached to the awning. The station closed entirely several months later. *Peter Tuffrey collection*

It passed through near-level countryside so earthworks were few, limited to shallow cuttings between Layerthorpe and Dunnington. Despite the absence of physical obstructions to influence its route, the line failed to serve any intermediate settlement conveniently, and Thorganby station was three-quarters of a mile from the diminutive village after which it was named. Since the carriage of agricultural goods on this line was of greater importance than passengers, farmers could be expected to get their produce to Thorganby and the other intermediate stations by horse and cart or newly developed motorised transport.

A most appealing style of building resembling a sports pavilion was used on the DVLR, with variations between stations. At Thorganby the single-storey building was on the single platform, east of the track. The structure was timber-framed with lath-and-plaster panels and a tiled roof. The twin gable-ends on the platform and entrance elevations were treated to a little 'Tudor' half-timbering,

Thorganby: By April 1984 the station has become somewhat shabby in the 20 years since it closed entirely. *Alan Young*

the decoration picked out by contrasting paint. On the platform side a recessed waiting area was provided under the roof and an awning was clasped between the two gables. The structure extended beyond the southern gable beneath a pitched roof (and decorated gable-end) adjoining a pent-roof on the eastern side. The red-brick two-storey station house stood apart,

Thorganby: The station building is in an advanced state of decay in April 2013; this is the platform (west) elevation. *Alan Young*

north of the platform and adjacent to the road. Although a single line passed through the station there was a loop immediately to the south, with four sidings to the east.

Prior to opening an agreement was made that locomotives, crew and stores would be hired from the NER, which provided two carriages. The first timetable showed three weekday southbound departures from Thorganby; there were three northbound, with an extra market train to York (Layerthorpe) on Monday and Saturday mornings. In July 1922 the timetable had become remarkably complex for such a modest undertaking. Southbound from Thorganby trains left at 9.52am (to Skipwith only from Tuesday to Friday, but extended to Cliff Common on Monday and Saturday); the Saturday-only 2.04pm went to Cliff Common; then trains at 4.52pm (Monday to Friday) and 6.32pm (Saturday only) ran to Skipwith. A Monday-to-Friday train was extended from Wheldrake (departing about 12.55pm) through Thorganby to Cliff Common, but only if parties of ten or more made prior arrangement to travel on it. Northbound there were three departures on Tuesday to Friday and four on Monday; three trains called on Saturday together with a further one that stopped by request to take up for York only. Smith (*Britain's Light Railways*, 1994) wonders whether the DVLR was trying to provide services that fitted local requirements or was trying to bludgeon local people into adapting to its ideals.

The DVLR continued its independent existence at the 1923 Grouping. To convey its diminishing number of passengers it bought a Ford-powered twin-unit bus with road-type wheels fitted with flanges; 36 passengers could be accommodated in the combined units. Turntables were installed at Skipwith and Layerthorpe permitting the units to be used singly. However, this novel form of traction failed to attract passengers to use the infrequent service and inconveniently sited stations, and in 1925 the DVLR carried only 18,430 passengers, who spent £664 on their fares. Growing competition from road transport brought an early end to DVLR passenger services on 31

Thorganby: This is the east elevation of the station building in April 2013. Damage to the panels reveals their lath-and-plaster construction. *Alan Young*

August 1926; they had lasted for just over 13 years. After formal closure to passengers, excursions continued to use the line until at least 1932. As late as 1960 the stations remained in good order, smartly painted despite their long period of closure to passengers.

Goods traffic remained buoyant for many years, and the remarkable fact that the line at one time had almost 5 miles of sidings is testament to this. A mustard gas factory at Cottingwith during the Second World War offered additional, unusual traffic; the weeds that engulfed the track were intentionally not removed, providing camouflage and rendering it safe from enemy air attack. The line was also used to carry materials to construct airfields at Elvington and Riccall. The DVLR escaped nationalisation in 1948 and continued to carry goods. Energetic General Managers Sidney Reading, from 1926 to 1963, and Jim Acklam from 1963 actively sought custom for the line, and consequently new agricultural and light industrial businesses added to the traffic. By the early 1950s the DVLR was using standard locomotives that could be seen on BR branch lines.

The entire line was retained for goods use until 31 December 1964, when the section from Wheldrake through Thorganby to Cliff Common closed; in its last years this part of the route contributed little traffic to the daily pick-up goods train, which rarely travelled as far south

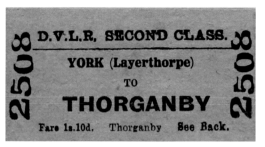

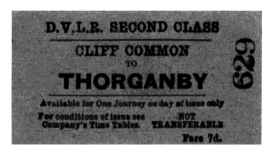

Thorganby: The station building and stationmaster's house are seen here, looking north in April 2013. *Alan Young*

as Cliff Common. The RCTS 'Derwent Valley Light Railway Tour' included a journey over the closed section on 9 and 16 January 1965, when two Mark 1 coaches were hauled by locomotive No D2111. The connection with the BR route at Cliff Common closed on 14 June 1965. The northern section of the route closed in stages, being cut back from Wheldrake to Elvington in May 1968 when it ceased to carry traffic for the Government 'buffer depot' for storage of food in case of national emergency, which had been built at Wheldrake in 1952. The line closed beyond Dunnington after the ICI liquid fertiliser plant beside Elvington station stopped using the rail facilities on 22 June 1973. However, the mechanised coal yard (opened in 1964) and Shell Mex fuel depot at Layerthorpe continued to help secure the line's viability.

In 1977-79 the remaining section hosted steam-hauled special trains in conjunction with the Friends of the newly opened National Railway Museum, and North Yorkshire County Council conducted a survey of local residents on whether a commuter service on the Derwent Valley could be introduced, but there was a lukewarm response. Although new grain traffic was acquired in 1979, this and the existing coal traffic soon slumped, and the last train between Layerthorpe and Dunnington ran on 27 September 1981. The tracks were lifted, but a short stretch was left in place at Murton thanks to the initiative of the DVLR Society, in association with the Yorkshire Museum of Farming, and advertised trains are operated for visitors. The building formerly at Wheldrake station has been re-erected here and is immaculately presented.

At Thorganby the station building survives in an exquisitely derelict state, but it is the intention of its owners to restore it.

Date opened	By October 1920
Location	On still-open line Selby/Goole-Hull line at Gibson Lane level crossing
Company on opening	North Eastern Railway
Date closed to passengers	8 July 1989
Date closed completely	8 July 1989
Company on closing	British Rail (Eastern Region)
Present state	Original platforms on each side of track are colonised by vegetation, but eastbound is heavily overgrown; later wooden eastbound platform removed
County	Yorkshire East Riding (now East Riding of Yorkshire)
OS grid ref	SE969257

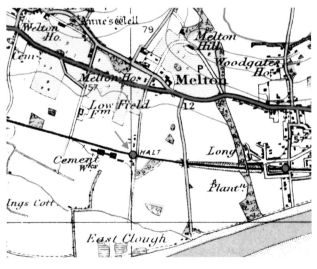

Melton Halt served the workforce of the Humber Portland Cement Company's lineside factory between Brough and Ferriby on the Selby-Hull route. Bairstow (1995) notes that the company informed the NER Traffic Committee in June 1920 that it would bear the cost of the halt's construction as well as its maintenance and any future alterations, should they be needed. It also guaranteed that a certain number of workmen's tickets would be purchased each week. The NER was to build the halt and provide stopping trains at suitable times for the workers.

The Hull & Selby Railway received the Royal Assent on 21 June 1836 and opened on 1 July 1840. It was notable for its minimal gradients and the longest straight stretch of permanent way in Britain – 18 miles between Selby and Brough. In 1903-04 the double-track route, shared by trains between Doncaster, Goole and Hull, was quadrupled east of Staddlethorpe (now known as Gilberdyke). On this section Melton Crossing Halt, as it was originally called, was located. Its two brick-built platforms were on the western side of Gibson Lane level crossing, served by the 'slow' lines (the two outer tracks). In later years a smelting works provided additional passengers for the halt. By February 1965 'Crossing' had been removed from the name. From May 1968 British Rail (Eastern Region) used the 'Halt' suffix only for untimetabled stations, and the tangerine North Eastern Region nameboards and later Corporate Identity nameplates on the lamps gave the name as 'Melton Halt'. By late 1971 the eastbound slow line had been removed and a short wooden platform with a standard BR Eastern Region 'bus shelter' was provided alongside the former fast line east of the level crossing, at first with a large Corporate Identity 'Melton' (not 'Halt') nameboard.

In common with many other 'works' halts, Melton was not advertised in public timetables. Despite this status, when closure was proposed it was subject to the normal TUCC procedure. Curiously at this late stage, from May 1987 the halt appeared in the public timetable with one train in each direction calling (at 07.32 westbound and 16.46 eastbound), indicated by

the footnote 'also stops at Melton Halt'. The halt closed on 8 July 1989. Following closure, the wooden eastbound platform was quickly removed; however, the original brick platforms remain, the eastbound one only just visible through the undergrowth. The adjacent Melton Lane signal box, which controls signalling for some distance towards Hull, also remains in place, but it is likely to disappear soon under the Gilberdyke-Ferriby resignalling project.

Left: **Melton Halt:** Looking east from the abandoned down (north) platform in August 1971, the tangerine-coloured BR(NE) nameboard has yet to be removed. When the down slow track was removed a timber platform was built to replace it beside the down fast track beyond the signal box and crossing. *John Mann*

Below: **Melton Halt:** The new down platform is seen in August 1971, with a 'bus shelter', Corporate Identity nameboard and modern electric lighting. *John Mann*

Melton Halt: The cement works served by the halt is in the background. The original up platform remains in use in April 1974, still with its BR(NE) nameboard and inconspicuous lighting, but no shelter. *Alan Young*

Left: **Melton Halt:** Looking west from a passing train in May 1978, the down platform – now with 'Melton Halt' signs – is in the foreground. Beyond the signal box and crossing the old down platform can be seen. *Alan Young*

Below left: **Melton Halt:** In July 2014 the up platform is being colonised by vegetation, and the cement works that it served has gone. *Mark Dyson*

Below: **Melton Halt:** Melton Lane signal box is still in use in July 2014. The former halt's up platform is in the distance. *Mark Dyson*

The Hull & Barnsley Railway, on which South Cave was described in an earlier section, came into being principally to carry freight traffic and to challenge the monopoly of the NER. In the 53 miles from Hull to Cudworth (near Barnsley), the only place of note directly served was Howden, whose population was about 2,000, and at its western end so little business was done that the H&BR's Denaby and Wath branches closed to passengers in 1903 and 1929 respectively, and the

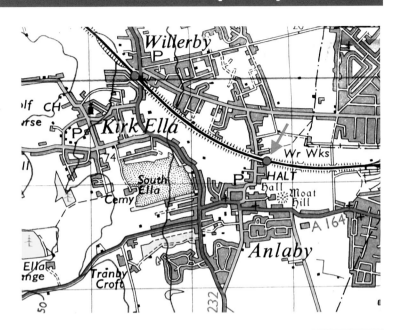

Date opened	8 April 1929
Location	East side of Wolfreton Road, Anlaby, opposite junction with road called Forty Steps
Company on opening	London & North Eastern Railway
Date closed to passengers	1 August 1955
Date closed completely	1 August 1955
Company on closing	British Railways (North Eastern Region)
Present state	Demolished and site now in residential use
County	Yorkshire East Riding (now East Riding of Yorkshire)
OS grid ref	TA037293

route west of South Howden lost its passenger services in 1932; the joint H&BR/GCR route through Sykehouse (described in *Lost Stations of Yorkshire: The West Riding*) failed to open to passenger traffic at all. Even the first 2½ miles from the H&BR's Hull terminus at Cannon Street were closed to passengers in 1924 when the LNER diverted trains to the main Paragon terminus. However, in 1929, at a time of falling receipts, the decision was taken by the LNER to open a halt at Springhead, 3½ miles from Hull Paragon.

In 1928 Anlaby Parish Council requested

that a station be provided by the LNER on the ex-H&BR route about a third of a mile north-east of the centre of Anlaby village, a little under a mile south-east of Willerby & Kirk Ella station. Although it was unusual in North East England for unstaffed halts to be provided for the general public, the LNER decided to construct one with facing 25-foot platforms, and tickets were made available in book form in local shops. The finances of the halt were gone into thoroughly, and it was judged that a 3d fare from Springhead Halt to Hull would allow the rail service to compete with buses, whose fares were 3½d to 4½d. These developments coincided with an initiative of Ralph Wedgwood, LNER Chief General Manager, to address the decline in suburban rail travel in the Hull area by introducing regular-interval services to attract more passengers, with new 'steam rail coaches' to make operation less expensive.

On the day when interval services began on Hull's local lines, 8 April 1929, Springhead Halt opened. The enhanced service on the ex-H&BR operated between Hull Paragon and South Howden, with 15 weekday return trains (three more than there had been in the previous year) and one on Sunday. In the 12 weeks ending 29 June 1929 Springhead Halt generated 3,840 single journeys to or from Hull. No shelters were provided on the platforms, which each boasted only a nameboard and two gas lamps. Local people knew the halt as 'Forty Steps' – the number that intending passengers had to climb to reach the platforms on the embankment.

By the winter of 1937-38 the timetable was erratic. There was no longer a service west of

Springhead Halt: On 18 March 1955 a Hull to North Cave train headed by 'G5' 0-4-4T No 67282 arrives at Springhead Halt to collect a solitary passenger. Two gas lamps and a nameboard are provided on each platform. This is one of the author's favourite railway photographs. *John Oxley*

South Howden, and about half of the trains did not call at Springhead. Six westbound trains called at the halt, the first being at 12.21pm on Monday to Friday, but as late as 4.34pm on Saturday. Eastbound there were six calls on Monday to Friday and five on Saturday. By 1943 fewer trains operated on the route, but most called at Springhead.

At nationalisation the line between Hull and South Howden was allocated to the North

Eastern Region, and Springhead was one of only six 'halts' listed in the timetable, North Eastrington on the same route being another. The 1950 service at Springhead amounted to six trains on Monday to Friday and seven on Saturday in each direction. In the face of dwindling bookings, Hull-South Howden closed on 1 August 1955, the final timetable (September 1954) indicating only four westbound calls at Springhead on Monday to Friday and six on Saturday, with five in the opposite direction (again six on Saturday). The June 1955 NE Region timetable book shows no service for Hull-South Howden, but tantalisingly says 'see further announcement' where the trains would usually be displayed.

The simple timber platforms at Springhead Halt were dismantled, leaving no trace. On 6 July 1964 the line through Springhead, which had been retained for freight as far west at Little Weighton, was closed. The bridge adjacent to the halt that had carried the line over Wolfreton Road was demolished in the 1970s, and the embankment on which the halt stood was removed. Houses and gardens now occupy its site.

Springhead Halt: This view, looking west, shows the halt soon after its closure in August 1955. The gas lamps and nameboards have been removed. *Courtesy of Hull & Barnsley Railway Stock Fund*

Springhead Halt: Looking east across Wolfreton Road in 2014, the railway bridge over the road was at this point and the halt was straight ahead, on an embankment that has been removed. The road name 'Forty Steps' (the sign is in the foreground) commemorates the stairways that led up to the halt. *Mark Dyson*

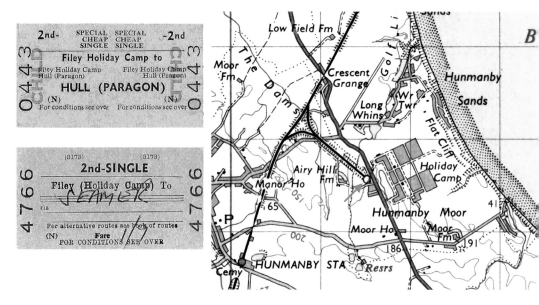

Date opened	10 May 1947 (official date)
Location	West of Moor Road (A165)
Company on opening	London & North Eastern Railway
Date closed to passengers	26 November 1977 (official date)
Date closed completely	26 November 1977
Company on closing	British Rail (Eastern Region)
Present state	Both platforms survive
County	Yorkshire North Riding (now North Yorkshire)
OS grid ref	TA115776

Billy (Sir William) Butlin opened his first British holiday camps at Skegness (1936) and Clacton (1938) for inexpensive, cheerful family holidays. A third camp at Filey was under way when the Second World War began, and Butlin shrewdly persuaded the War Ministry to complete its construction to serve as the RAF Hunmanby Moor training facility. When peace returned in 1945 Butlin reclaimed the camp, and its first guests arrived in July 1945. Work began on a branch railway off the Hull-Scarborough line to serve it; this was at the insistence of the local council, which expected arrangements to be made with the LNER to provide 'a siding near the site where visitors to the proposed camp could detrain'.

The branch left the main line at Royal Oak North and South junctions and was about three-quarters of a mile in length. Filey Holiday Camp station had two 300-yard island platforms constructed of reinforced concrete panels. Temporary timber buildings allowed the station to open as early as possible, giving way soon to an unadorned single-storey brick structure that provided basic facilities for staff and passengers. There was no booking or enquiry office at the station, but passengers could use the railway office in the camp for such business. Concrete lamp standards, with the electric lamp in an LNER 'mint imperial' shade within a hoop – a style designed for island platforms – were accompanied by

Filey Holiday Camp: On 6 March 1965 a large number of passengers leave a train that has arrived behind a Class 'K1' 2-6-0. *John Mann collection*

running-in boards, also on concrete stanchions. Small LNER nameplates were fixed to the lamps. At first passengers left the station by a staircase adjoining the concourse, then crossed the main Scarborough-Bridlington road, in the days before suitcases had wheels and had to be carried. Eventually a tunnel was opened under the road, with one lane for pedestrians and two for vehicles, and a 'trolley train' was provided between the station and the camp for patrons and their luggage.

The station came into use before its formal opening. On 21 October 1946 a train ran to publicise the camp, on which Butlin accompanied 400 'celebrities' in 'Yorkshire Pullman' coaches to attend a performance of Puccini's *La Bohème* in the Viennese Ballroom. The day was marred by a fire in one of the coaches, which delayed the train from King's Cross for 2 hours. On 10 May 1947 the official opening took place when Lord Middleton, Lord Lieutenant of the East Riding, unveiled one of the station nameboards.

Filey Holiday Camp: The station building, looking north-west in June 1974. *John Mann*

Although intended for passenger use, pick-up goods trains visited the branch to deliver supplies to the camp or to the station itself. Passenger use was largely confined to summer Saturdays, and station staff were seconded from Hull, but for midweek workings the stationmaster at Filey released staff to attend the passengers. The two Royal Oak signal boxes

Filey Holiday Camp: A 'mint imperial' lamp and nameplate of LNER vintage, also photographed in June 1974. *John Mann*

and that at the camp station opened only when the branch was in use and were operated by relief signalmen.

The summer 1955 timetable shows Saturday-only trains that departed for Newcastle, King's Norton, York, Sheffield Victoria, Manchester (London Road and Victoria), London King's Cross, Leeds City and Edinburgh Waverley; the last departure of the day was at 11.35am. The popularity of the camp increased until in 1975 it welcomed 173,000 guests. In the summer of 1969 the author spent a not entirely enjoyable time working in the camp's kitchen, arriving and departing on weekdays when, sadly, there were no trains running. Despite its growing clientele, use of the camp station declined as more guests travelled by car; in 1955 a little over half used the station but in 1975 the figure was only 7% (12,400 passengers). With fewer trains to accommodate from April 1972 the trackwork and signalling were simplified and rails were removed from the north-east island platform (numbered 3 and 4). In the 1975 season destinations of through trains included Bradford Exchange, Liverpool Lime Street, Newcastle, Sheffield and Leicester. In July and August 1976 a locally advertised experimental Wednesday-only service ran to and from Hull.

Filey Holiday Camp: A June 1974 view of the trackwork immediately north-west of the station. *John Mann*

Although Dr Beeching advocated the run-down of extra summer trains to holiday resorts, which required the maintenance of vast numbers of coaches for only a few weeks' use, Filey Holiday Camp station was not threatened with closure. However, the 'Network for Development' plan (1967) proposed the closure to passengers of the Hull-Bridlington line – as noted in the Flamborough section above – and complete closure from Bridlington to Seamer, and thus of the camp branch. BR brushed off objections to the branch closure, asserting that guests reached the camp by bus from Filey station before the branch opened,

Filey Holiday Camp: A British Rail 'Corporate Identity' running-in board in June 1974. *John Mann*

Filey Holiday Camp: The 'trolley train', also photographed in June 1974, conveyed passengers and their luggage to and from the camp through a tunnel under the A165 road. *John Mann*

and that they could do so from Scarborough station (as the author did in 1969). The closure of Hull-Scarborough was refused, but a fresh proposal was made in 1976 to close Filey Holiday Camp station. On 17 September 1977 the last train left the station, at the end of the holiday season; closure was announced on 26 October 1977 and it took effect a month later

on 26 November.

As the lure of warm overseas holiday destinations increased, the windswept cliff top of Filey lost appeal, and the camp closed in 1983. Although it briefly reopened as Amtree Park in 1986, it was demolished between 1988 and 2003. It has been outlived by the disused station, where the platforms survive, together with access steps and lamp standards. The site is now used for the storage of dumped agricultural machinery and old circus lorries.

Filey Holiday Camp: In March 1987 the station building has been removed and the platforms are in use for storing bales of hay. *Alan Young*

DISUSED STATIONS
Closed Railway Stations In the UK

Since its launch in 2004, *Subterranea Britannica's* DISUSED STATIONS web site has become established as one of the most comprehensive online photographic records of closed stations in the UK with a wide selection of 'then' and 'now' photographs.

Each station page includes a selection of archive pictures showing the station before closure and the site as it appears today plus Ordnance Survey maps, tickets, timetables and a brief history of the station or line.

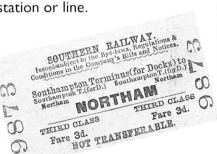

With over 6,000 closed stations in the UK this will be a very long term project, but with 2010 stations covered (as of September 2015) we have already made a serious dent in that number. However there is still a long way to go. DISUSED STATIONS welcomes contributions from anyone, any station, any line, any period in time but, if you aren't the photographer please make sure you have the copyright owner's permission before sending photographs for inclusion on the website.

Visit us at www.disused-stations.org.uk/sites.shtml
- you won't be disappointed.

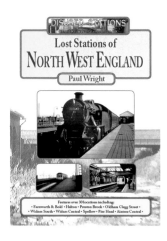

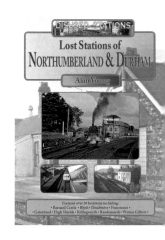

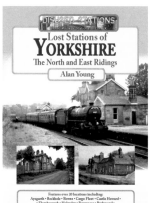

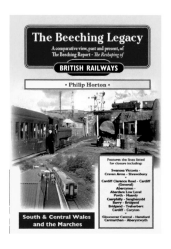

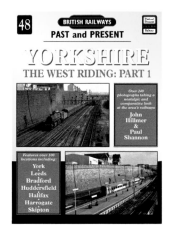

Available through all good booksellers or by mail order from:

The NOSTALGIA *Collection*
Silver Link Publishing Ltd •The Trundle • Ringstead Road •
Great Addington • Kettering • Northants • NN14 4BW